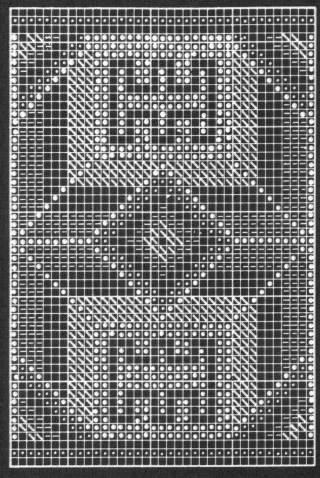

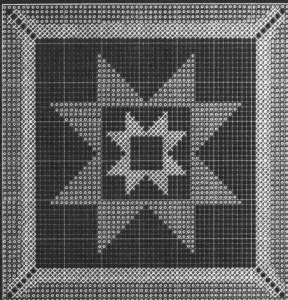

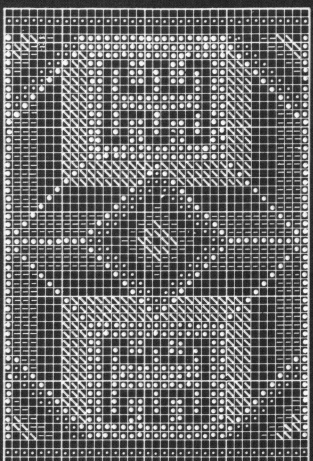

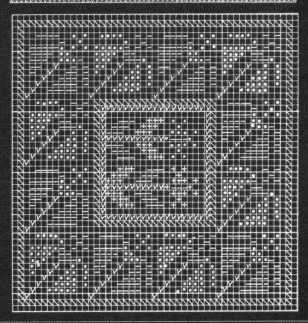

KNITTING & CROCHET
From McCall's Needlework and Crafts

KNITTING & CROCHET

from
McCall's
Needlework & Crafts

SEDGEWOOD™PRESS
NEW YORK

For Sedgewood™ Press
Editorial Director, Sedgewood™ Press: *Jane Ross*
Project Director: *Wendy Rieder*
Managing Editor: *Gale Kremer*
Designer: *H. Roberts*
Production Manager: *Bill Rose*

All photographs in this book are the property of McCall's
Needlework & Crafts magazine.

Distributed in the Trade by Van Nostrand Reinhold

ISBN 0-442-28200-1

Library of Congress Catalog Number 83-51234

Manufactured in the United States of America

CONTENTS

INTRODUCTION

THE KNITTING AND CROCHET projects assembled in this volume have been chosen for their beauty, practicality, and variety in both design and difficulty. Each sweater and accessory has a distinctive style or pattern that sets it apart from the ordinary, but all are chosen for their long-term value in a wardrobe or as a belonging. You are sure to find something suitable for almost anyone or any occasion, from a dressy cardigan to an outfit for the ski slopes, or a charming suit or a blanket for an infant.

The cardigans, vests, and pullovers are made with all kinds of differently-shaped necklines. They are also worked in a wide variety of patterns and textures with different weights and types of yarn so there is choice enough to please both sexes, adult as well as child, for all seasons. The accessories, which always make welcome gifts, include a number of hats, mittens, gloves, scarves, afghans, and stoles, as well as pillows, rugs, and totes for something a little more unusual.

Children will especially love the topsy-turvy and Mother Goose dolls. The former, turn from storybook characters into animals when tipped upside down, and the latter are accompanied by the things with which they are associated in their rhymes, such as a haystack for Little Boy Blue.

Some of the projects, such as the garter stitch cardigan or the openwork double-crochet pullover can be made both easily and quickly with simple stitches and heavy yarn. Others, like the Aran sweaters and the lacy crocheted cardigans require more time and experience. But, regardless of your skill level, there is an ample diversity of patterns from which to choose.

To make the instructions as clear and meaningful as possible, a lengthy section on knitting and crochet basics has been included at the back of the book. There, in addition to some embroidery stitches required in various projects, you will find illustrations of all the common knitting and crochet stitches and techniques required in the book. You will also find instructions for following knitting and crochet directions, common abbreviations, and explanations of how to check your gauge and block your work. Whether you are knitting or crocheting, always remember to check your gauge periodically, as directed, to avoid a great deal of extra effort and ensure successful results.

Whichever projects you choose to make, you are sure to please the beneficiary of your efforts, whomever it might be, for the designs you find here are all endowed with a certain timelessness of style and classic beauty that will remain appealing for years on end.

PART I
KNITTING FOR THE WHOLE FAMILY

The following collection of sweater patterns offers something to please everyone— you, the man in your life, a child, a relative, or a friend. The styles include a variety of cardigans, pullovers, turtlenecks, and vests, some of which are accompanied by such accessories as mittens, hats, scarves, and knee socks. The patterns vary in complexity to suit knitters of different skill levels and the assortment of designs incorporates details like cables, argyles, and various motifs such as flowers, hearts, and snowflakes, which provide added beauty and interest to the garments.

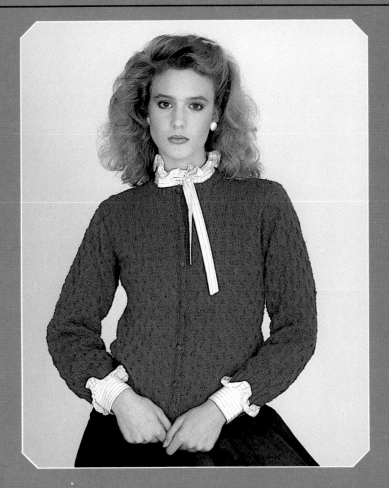

An Elegantly-fashioned Shadow Cable Cardigan

Perfect for any season, this finely textured cable cardigan provides a dressy look with warmth knit in.

SIZES: Directions for small size (8–10). Changes for medium size (12–14) are in parentheses.

Body Bust Size: 31½″–32½″ (34″–36″)

Blocked Bust Size (closed): 35″ (39″)

MATERIALS: Sport yarn, 14 (15) 50-gram (1¾-oz.) balls. 29″ circular knitting needles, Nos. 4 and 6 (3½ and 4¼ mm). Dp or cable needle. Seven (eight) buttons. Three stitch holders.

GAUGE: 6 sts = 1″; 7 rows = 1″ (No. 6 needles, pat st). To save time, take time to check your gauge.

PATTERN (worked on a multiple of 8 sts, plus 4)

Row 1 (right side): Knit.

Row 2: Purl.

Row 3: K 2, * with yarn to back, sl 2, k 6, repeat from * across, end last repeat k 8.

Row 4: P 8, * with yarn to front, sl 2, p 6, repeat from * across, end last repeat p 2.

Row 5: K 2, * sl 2 sts onto dp needle and hold in front of work, k next 2 sts, k 2 sts from dp needle, k 4, repeat from * across, end last repeat k 6.

Row 6: Purl.

Row 7: Knit.

Row 8: Purl.

Row 9: * K 6, with yarn to back, sl 2, repeat from * across, end k 4.

Row 10: P 4, * with yarn to front, sl 2, p 6, repeat from * across.

Row 11: K 6, * sl 2 onto dp needle and hold in front of work, k next 2 sts, k 2 sts from dp needle, k 4, repeat from * across.

Row 12: Purl. Repeat rows 1–12 for pat.

CARDIGAN BODY: Beg at lower edge of fronts and back, with No. 4 needle, cast on 181 (201) sts. Do not join; work back and forth in ribbing as follows:

Row 1 (right side): K 1, * p 1, k 1, repeat from * across.

Row 2: P 1, * k 1, p 1, repeat from * across. Repeat these 2 rows for 1¾″, inc 23 (27) sts evenly spaced across last row, end wrong side—204 (228) sts. Change to No. 6 needle. Working back and forth, work in pat until piece measures 13½″ (14½″) from start, end wrong side. Piece above ribbing should measure 34″ (38″) wide.

Divide For Underarm: Keeping to pat, work 39 (43) sts (right front), sl these sts on a holder, bind off next 22 (26) sts for right underarm, work 82 (90) sts (back), sl these sts on a holder, bind off next 22 (26) sts for left underarm, work 39 (43) sts (left front).

Left Front: Work in pat until armhole measures 5¼″ (5½″) above bound-off sts, end center edge.

Shape Neck: Work 8 (9) sts, sl these sts on a holder, finish row—31 (34) sts. Dec 1 st at neck edge every row 3 (4) times, then every other row twice—26 (28) sts. Work even until armhole measures 7¼″ (7¾″) above bound-off sts, end arm side.

Shape Shoulder: Bind off 9 (10) sts at beg of arm side twice, 8 sts once.

Right Front: Sl sts from holder to No. 6 needle; join yarn at underarm. Work same as for left front, reversing shaping.

Back: Sl sts from holder to No. 6 needle; join yarn at left underarm. Work in pat until armholes measure 7¼″ (7¾″) above bound-off sts.

Shape Shoulders: Bind off 9 (10) sts at beg of next 4 rows, 8 sts next 2 rows. Sl remaining 30 (34) sts on a holder.

SLEEVES: Beg at lower edge with No. 4 needle, cast on 43 (47) sts. Work back and forth in ribbing same as for back for 1¾″, inc 25 (29) sts evenly spaced across last row, end wrong side—68 (76) sts. Change to No. 6 needle. Working in pat, inc 1 st each side every 10th row 8 times, working added sts into pat—84 (92) sts. Work even until piece measures 17″ (17½″) from start. Piece above last inc row should measure 14″ (15¼″) wide. Mark each side of last row for start of underarm. Work even until piece measures 2½″ (2¾″) above markers. Bind off loosely.

Left Center Band: With No. 4 needles, cast on 5 sts. Work in ribbing of k 1, p1 until piece when slightly stretched, measures same as left front edge. Sl sts on a safety pin. Sew band to left front edge.

With pins, mark position of 6 (7) buttons evenly spaced on left center band; first button ½″ above lower edge, 7th (8th) button will be in neckband.

BUTTONHOLES: From right side, k 1, p 1, yo, k 2 tog, k 1.

Next Row: Work in ribbing across.

Right Center Band: Work same as for left center band, forming buttonholes opposite markers. Sew band to right front edge.

FINISHING: Block pieces. Sew shoulder seams. Sew sleeve seams from lower edge to markers. With sleeve markers at center of underarm, sew side of sleeves to bound-off underarm sts; sew bound-off sts of sleeve to armhole edge.

Neckband: From right side, with No. 4 needle, work in ribbing across sts of right front center band, k across 8 (9) sts on right front holder, pick up and k 10 sts on right front neck edge, k across sts on back holder, pick up and k 11 sts on left front neck edge, k across 8 (9) sts on left front holder, work in ribbing across sts of left front center band— 77 (83) sts. Work back and forth in ribbing for 3 rows, forming buttonhole on right center band on 2nd row. Bind off in ribbing same tension as sts.

Sew on buttons.

A Pair of
Blossom-patterned Pullovers

Both of these soft-colored sweaters are distinguished by their spring look as well as by their sophisticated design. Though the patterns may appear difficult, the sweaters are worked entirely in the stockinette stitch, except for the ribbing; they are also knit from the top down.

Placket Neck Pullover

SIZES: Directions for small size (6–8). Changes for medium size (10–12) and large size (14) are in parentheses.

Body Bust Size: 30½"–31½" (32½"–34"; 36")

Blocked Bust Size: 34½" (37½"–40")

MATERIALS: Knitting worsted, 4 (5–6) 4-oz. balls ecru (A), 1 ball each of peach (B) and avocado (C). 29" circular needles, Nos. 6 and 8 (4¼ and 5 mm). Four stitch holders. Three buttons.

GAUGE: 9 sts = 2"; 6 rows = 1" (No. 8 needles).

Note: Pullover is worked from neck to lower edge.

Pattern Notes: Always change colors on wrong side, picking up new strand from under dropped strand. Carry unused colors across loosely; if more than 3 sts between colors, twist strands after every 3rd st. Cut and join colors when necessary.

Inc Notes: To inc 1 st in first or last st, k in front and back of same st. To make raglan inc, place right-hand needle behind left-hand needle, insert right needle in stitch below next st, k this st, then k st above it.

YOKE: Beg at neck edge, with A and No. 8 needle, cast on 48 (50–52) sts. Do not join; work back and forth as follows:

Row 1 (wrong side): P 3 (front), put a marker on needle, p 8 (right sleeve), put a marker on needle, p 26 (28–30) sts (back), put a marker on needle, p 8 (left sleeve), put a marker on needle, p 3 (front)—4 markers.

Row 2 (right side): * K to 1 st before marker, inc 1 st (see Inc Notes), sl marker, inc 1 st, repeat from * 3 times, k across—8 sts inc.

Row 3: Inc 1 st, p across, inc 1 st in last st— 2 sts inc. Working in stockinette st (k 1 row, p 1 row) repeat row 2 every k row 23 (25–27) times more; **at the same time,** inc 1 st each side every p row 2 (3–4) times more, then inc 1 st each side of next row, then cast on 3 sts at end of next 2 rows— 102 (114–126) sts.

Continue to work raglan incs until you have 110 (130–150) sts, end p row.

Row 14 (18–22): * K 2 C, k 2 B, repeat from * to 1 st before marker; with C, k st below next st; with B, k st above it (1 st inc), sl marker; with B, k st below next st; with C, k st above it (1 st inc); working 2 sts B, 2 sts C, continue to inc 1 st before and after each marker, end 2 C sts—118 (138–158) sts.

Next Row: * P 2 B, p 2 C, repeat from * across, end p 2 B. Continuing to work raglan incs, with A, work 4 rows, dec 1 st in center back of last row—133 (153–173) sts.

PATTERN

Row 1: Continuing to work raglan incs, following chart, k from A to B, from C to D, from E to center st; then back on same row to E, from D to C, from B to A.

Row 2: Following chart, p from A to B, from C to D, from E to center st, then back on same row to E, from D to C, from B to A. Working appropriate pat row, work to top of chart (row 27), end k row—245 (265–285) sts. With A only, work 2 rows, end k row—253 (273–293) sts. All raglan incs are completed. Do not turn; cast on 6 sts at end of last rnd—259 (279–299) sts.

Joining Rnd: Put a marker on needle for start of rnd; from right side, k across left front, sleeve, inc 1 st at start of back, k across back, sleeve, right front—260 (280–300) sts.

Next Rnd: K around, inc 1 st before and after each raglan marker—268 (288–308) sts.

Next Rnd: * K 2 B, k 2 C, repeat from * around.

Next Rnd: * K 2 C, k 2 B, repeat from * around.

Divide Work: Sl 35 (38–41) sts (left front) on a holder, sl next 58 (62–66) sts (left sleeve) on a holder, sl next 76 (82–88) sts (back) on a holder, leave next 58 (62–66) sts (right sleeve) on needle, sl last 41 (44–47) sts (right front) on a holder.

Right Sleeve: With A, from right side, cast on 1 (2–3) sts, k across right sleeve, cast on 1

(2–3) sts—60 (66–72) sts. Working back and forth, p 1 row, k 1 row, p 1 row.

PATTERN

Row 1 (right side): K 3 A, * k 1 C, k 5 A, repeat from * across, end last repeat k 2 A.

Rows 2–5: With A, (p 1 row, k 1 row) twice.

Row 6: * P 5 A, p 1 C, repeat from * across.

Rows 7–10: With A, (k 1 row, p 1 row) twice. Repeat rows 1–10 for pat, until sleeve measures 14″ from start, or 3″ less than desired sleeve length; **at the same time,** keeping to pat as established, dec 1 st each side every 10th row 7 times, end k row—46 (52–58) sts. With A, p 1 row, dec 2 (4–6) sts evenly spaced—44 (48–52) sts.

Next Row: * K 2 B, k 2 C, repeat from * across.

Next Row: * P 2 B, p 2 C, repeat from * across. Change to No 6 needle. With A, k across, dec 2 (4–6) sts evenly spaced across—42 (44–46) sts. Work in ribbing of k 1, p 1 for 2½″. Bind off in ribbing same tension as sts.

Left Sleeve: From right side, sl sts of left sleeve to No. 8 needle—58 (62–66) sts. Work same as for right sleeve.
Sew sleeve seams.

Body: From right side, with No. 8 needle and A, k across sts of left front, pick up and k 2 sts on left underarm, k across back sts, pick up and k 2 sts on right underarm, k across right front—156 (168–180) sts.

PATTERN

Rnds 1–3: Knit.

Rnd 4: * K 5 A, k 1 C, repeat from * around.

Rnds 5–8: With A, knit.

Rnd 9: K 2 A, * k 1 C, k 5 A, repeat from * around, end last repeat k 3 A.

Rnds 10–13: With A, knit. Repeat rnds 4–13 until piece measures 9½″ from underarm, dec 8 sts evenly spaced around last rnd—148 (160–172) sts.

14

Placket-Neck Pullover Chart

COLOR
KEY

☐ A
▣ B
◨ C

center stitch

Next Rnd: * K 2 B, k 2 C, repeat from * around.

Next Rnd: * K 2 C, k 2 B, repeat from * around. Change to No. 6 needle. Work in ribbing of k 1, p 1 for 3″. Bind off in ribbing same tension as sts.

Neckband: From right side, with A and No. 6 needle, pick up and k 72 (76–80) sts around neck edge. Work in ribbing of k 1, p 1 for 1″. Bind off in ribbing same tension as sts.

Left Center Band: From right side, with A and No. 6 needle, pick up and k 38 (40–42) sts on left front edge. Work in ribbing of k 1, p 1 for 1″. Bind off in ribbing.

Right Center Band: Pick up and work same as for left band for 3 rows, end lower edge.

Next Row: Working in ribbing, work 8 sts, * bind off next 2 sts, work next 11 (12–13) sts from bound-off sts, repeat from * once, bind off next 2 sts, finish row.

Next Row: Work in ribbing as established, cast on 2 sts over bound-off sts. Work 2 rows even. Bind off in ribbing.

FINISHING: Run in yarn ends on wrong side. Lap right center band over left center band; weave lower edge of bands to cast-on sts. Steam-press lightly. Sew on buttons.

Bateau Neck Pullover

SIZES: Directions for small size (8–10). Changes for medium size (12–14) and large size (16–18) are in parentheses.

Body Bust Size: 31½″–32½″ (34″–36″; 38″–40″)

Blocked Bust Size: 36″ (39½″–43″)

MATERIALS: Knitting worsted, 3 (3–4) 4-oz. balls ecru (A), 2 balls each of peach (B) and med. avocado (C). Knitting needles, Nos. 6 and 8 (4¼ and 5 mm).

GAUGE: 9 sts = 2″; 6 rows = 1″ (No. 8 needles).

Note: Back and front are worked from upper to lower edge; sleeve from armhole to lower edge.

Pattern Notes: Always change colors on wrong side, picking up new strand from under dropped strand. Carry unused colors across loosely; if more than 3 sts between colors, twist strands after every 3rd st. Always bring unused color to end of row and twist before beginning next row. Cut and join colors when necessary.

PULLOVER BACK: Beg at upper edge (see Note), with C and No. 8 needles, cast on 45 (47–49) sts.

Neck Facing: P 1 row. Working in stockinette st (k 1 row, p 1 row), dec 1 st each side every row 4 times, end p row—37 (39–41) sts. Cast on 21 (25–28) sts at beg of next 2 rows for shoulders, end p row—79 (89–97) sts.

PATTERN

Row 1 (right side): Following Chart 1, k from A to B once, from B to C across.

Row 2: P from C to B to last st, from B to A once.

Rows 3–12: Repeat rows 1 and 2, 5 times.

Row 13: With A, knit.

Row 14: With A, purl.

Row 15: Following Chart 2, k from A to B once, from B to C to last 7 (7–6) sts, from C to D once.

Row 16: Following Chart 2, p from D to C once, from C to B to last 2 (2–1) sts, from B to A once.

Rows 17–23: Repeat last 2 rows to top of chart, end k row.

Row 24: With A, purl.

Row 25: With A, knit.

Row 26: Repeat row 2.

Rows 27–36: Repeat rows 1 and 2, 5 times.

Row 37: Repeat row 1.

Row 38: With A, purl.

Row 39: With A, knit.

Row 40: Following Chart 2, p from A to B once, from B to C to last 7 (7–6) sts, from C to D once.

Row 41: Following Chart 2, k from D to C once, from C to B to last 2 (2–1) sts, from B to A once.

Rows 42–48: Repeat last 2 rows to top of chart, end p row.

Row 49: With A, knit.

Row 50: With A, purl. Repeat rows 1–50 for pat once, then repeat rows 1 and 2 until piece measures 21″ from last cast-on sts (shoulders), end wrong side. Change to No. 6 needles. With A, work in ribbing of k 1, p 1 for 2″. Bind off in ribbing same tension as sts.

FRONT: Work same as for back.
   Sew shoulder seams. Mark 7½″ (8″–8½″) each side of shoulder seam for underarm.

SLEEVES Beg at underarm marker, from right side, with C and No. 8 needles, pick up and k 65 (69–73) sts on armhole edge, end at underarm marker.

Rows 1–14: Work same as for back pat rows 1–14.

Row 15: Following Chart 3, k from A to B once, from B to C to last 10 (7–9) sts, from C to D once.

Row 16: Following Chart 3, p from D to C once, from C to B to last 5 (2–4) sts, from B to A once.

Rows 17–23: Repeat last 2 rows to top of chart, end k row.

Row 24: With A, purl.

Row 25: With A, knit, dec 1 st each side—63 (67–71) sts. Keeping to pat as established, dec

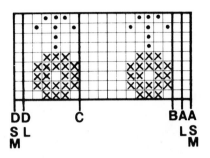

A
B
C

Bateau-Neck Pullover: Chart 1

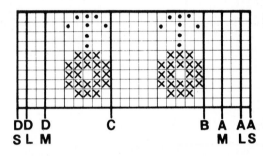

Bateau-Neck Pullover: Chart 2

Bateau-Neck Pullover: Chart 3

1 st each side every 25 rows twice more—59 (63–67) sts. Repeat pat rows 1 and 2 until sleeve measures 15″ from start or 3″ less than desired sleeve length, end wrong side.

Next Row: With A, k across, dec 18 sts evenly spaced—41 (45–49) sts. Change to No. 6 needles. Work in ribbing of k 1, p 1 for 3″. Bind off in ribbing same tension as sts. Work 2nd sleeve in same manner.

FINISHING: Run in yarn ends on wrong side. Sew side and sleeve seams. Fold neck facing to wrong side; hem in place. Steam-press lightly.

A Sporty
Scoop-necked Argyle Pullover

Scoop-necked sweaters are always versatile and especially pretty because they show off so many different blouses and scarves. The argyle pattern of this one makes each combination all the more interesting and striking.

SIZES: Directions for size 8. Changes for sizes 10, 12, 14 and 16 are in parentheses.

Body Bust Size: 31½" (32½"–34"–36"–38")

Blocked Bust Size: 31½" (33"–34½"–36½"–38")

MATERIALS: Knitting worsted, 4 4-oz. skeins rust (R), 2 4-oz. skeins pine green (P), 1 4-oz. skein each of leaf green (L) and yellow (Y). Knitting needles, Nos. 5 and 8. Set of bobbins. Large-eyed tapestry needle.

GAUGE: 9 sts = 2"; 6 rows = 1" (argyle pat, No. 8 needles).

Notes: Front argyle pat is worked in stockinette st (k 1 row, p 1 row); remainder of sweater is worked in ribbing of k 1, p 1. Diamond pat is worked with bobbins; L and Y lines are embroidered in double duplicate stitch when front is completed.

Argyle Pattern Notes: Use a separate bobbin for each color change. Always change colors on wrong side, picking up new strand from under dropped strand.

SWEATER BACK: Beg at lower edge with R and No. 5 needles, cast on 70 (74–78–82–86) sts. Work in ribbing of k 1, p 1 for 4½". Change to No. 8 needles. Working in ribbing as established, work even until piece measures 13" (13"–13½"–13½"–14") from start or desired length to underarm.

Shape Armholes: Bind off 5 (5–5–6–6) sts at beg of next 2 rows. Dec 1 st each side every other row 4 (5–6–6–7) times—52 (54–56–58–60) sts. Work even until armholes measure 6½" (6¾"–7"–7¼"–7½") above first bound-off sts.

Shape Shoulders: Bind off 4 (4–4–4–5) sts at beg of next 4 (4–2–2–2) rows, 5 sts next 2 (2–4–4–4) rows. Bind off remaining 26 (28–28–30–30) sts.

FRONT: Work same as for back until piece measures 4½" from start. Change to No. 8 needles. Working in stockinette st (k 1 row, p 1 row), work 2 rows R, 2 rows P, end p row.

PATTERN

Row 1: Following chart, k from A to B once, from B to C twice, from C to D once.

Row 2: P from D to C once, from C to B twice, from B to A once. Continue in this manner to top of chart. Repeat the 26 rows of chart for pat until piece measures 11½" (11½"–12"–12"–12½") from start or 1½" less than back to underarm. Piece above ribbing should measure 15¾" (16½"–17¼"–18¼"–19") wide.

Shape Neck: Keeping to pat, work 30 (32–34–36–38) sts, drop yarn; join another strand of color to be used, bind off center 10 sts, finish row—30 (32–34–36–38) sts each

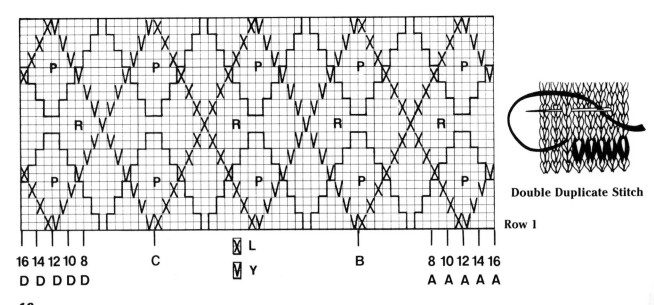

Double Duplicate Stitch

Row 1

16 14 12 10 8   C   L   B   8 10 12 14 16

D D D D D   Y   A A A A A

side. Keeping to pat as established, working on both sides at once, bind off 2 sts at beg of each neck edge 4 times. Dec 1 st at each neck edge every other row 0 (1–1–2–2) times; **at the same time,** when piece measures same as back to underarm, bind off 5 (5–5–6–6) sts at beg of each arm side once. Dec 1 st at each arm side every other row 4 (5–6–6–7) times— 13 (13–14–14–15) sts each side. Work even until armholes measure same as back.

Shape Shoulders: Bind off 4 (4–4–4–5) sts at beg of each arm side 2 (2–1–1–1) times, 5 sts 1 (1–2–2–2) times.

SLEEVES: Beg at lower edge with R and No. 5 needles, cast on 36 (36–38–38–38) sts. Work in ribbing of k 1, p 1 for 2″. Change to No. 8 needles. Inc 1 st each side of next row, then every 1″ 13 (14–14–15–16) times, working added sts into ribbing—64 (66–68–70–72) sts. Work even until piece measures 17″ (17″–17½″–18″–18½″) from start or desired length to underarm.

Shape Cap: Bind off 5 (5–5–6–6) sts at beg of next 2 rows. Dec 1 st each side every other row 4 (5–6–6–7) times. Bind off 2 sts at beg of every row 16 times. Bind off remaining 14 sts.

NECKBAND: With R and No. 5 needles, cast on 132 (136–140–144–148) sts. Work in ribbing of k 1, p 1 for 1″. Bind off in ribbing same tension as sts.

FINISHING: Run in yarn ends on wrong side. Following chart, beg on pat row 1 at lower edge of front pat, embroider L and Y lines in double duplicate stitch, working each st over 2 rows of knitting to top of chart (see drawing below). Continue to upper edge of front, moving duplicate st over 1 st every other row. Sew shoulder seams; sew in sleeves. Sew side and sleeve seams. Pin cast-on edge of neckband over neck edge, with ends at center back. Weave ends tog; sew neckband in place. Steam-press argyle pat lightly; do not press ribbing.

A Warm and Wintry-looking Cardigan and Turtleneck in Soft Neutrals

These handsome winter-weight sweaters are knit with double yarn. The cardigan is knit entirely of garter stitches, except for the collar and ribbing. The turtleneck is distinguished by the design of its deep yoke and dropped shoulders.

Garter Stitch Cardigan

SIZES: Directions for small size (6–8). Changes for medium size (10–12) and large size (14) are in parentheses.

Body Bust Size: 30½″–31½″ (32½″–34″; 36″)

Finished Bust Size (closed): 32½″ (35½″–38½″)

MATERIALS: Knitting worsted, 5 100-gram skeins each of gray (A) and natural (B). Knitting needles, Nos. 10½ and 13. Crochet hook, size I. One stitch holder. Six buttons.

GAUGE: 5 sts = 2″ (Double strand of yarn, No. 13 needles).

Note: Entire cardigan is worked in garter st with double strand of yarn throughout. Cut and join colors as needed.

CARDIGAN BACK: Beg at lower edge, with double strand of A (see Note) and No. 10½ needles, cast on 40 (44–48) sts. Work in ribbing of k 1, p 1 for 2½″. Change to No. 13 needles. Work in garter st (k each row) until piece measures 4¾″ (5″–5¼″) above ribbing. With one strand each of A and B, work even until piece measures 10¼″ (10½″–10¾″) from start. Piece above ribbing should measure 16″ (17½″–19¼″) wide.

Shape Armholes: Bind off 4 sts at beg of next 2 rows—32 (36–40) sts. Work even until piece measures 12½″ (13″–13½″) from start. With double strand B, work even until armholes measure 6¾″ (7″–7″) above first bound-off sts.

Shape Neck and Shoulders: K 11 (13–15), drop yarn, sl center 10 sts on a holder; join double strand of B, finish row—11 (13–15) sts each side. Working on both sides at once, with separate strands of B, dec 1 st at beg of each neck edge twice—9 (11–13) sts each side. Work even until armholes measure 8¼″ (8½″–8¾″) above first bound-off sts. Bind off.

RIGHT FRONT: Beg at lower edge, with double strand A and No. 10½ needles, cast on 22 (24–26) sts. Work in ribbing of k 1, p 1 for 1″ (1½″–2″). Mark end of last row for center edge.

Next Row (buttonhole row): K 1, p 1, yo, k 2 tog, finish row. Work in ribbing until piece measures 2½″ from start. Change to No. 13 needles. Working in garter st, changing colors same as for back, form buttonholes at center edge every 3″ 5 times more; **at the same time,** when piece measures same as back to underarm, bind off 4 sts at beg of side edge once—18 (20–22) sts. Work even until armhole measures 6″ (6½″–6¾″) above bound-off sts.

Shape Neck: Bind off 6 sts at beg of center edge once. Dec 1 st at same edge every row 3 times—9 (11–13) sts. Work even until armhole measures same as back. Bind off.

LEFT FRONT: Work same as for right front, omitting buttonholes; pat is reversible.

SLEEVES: Beg at lower edge, with double strand A and No. 10½ needles, cast on 26 (28–28) sts. Work in ribbing of k 1, p 1 for 2″, inc 1 st each side of last row—28 (30–30) sts. Change to No. 13 needles. Work in garter st, inc 1 st each side every 2½″ 6 times more; **at the same time,** when piece measures 11″ (11½″–11½″) from start, work with 1 strand each of A and B until piece measures 16¼″ (17″–17½″) from start, then work with double strand of B until piece measures 18″ (18½″–18½″) from start or desired length to underarm—40 (42–42) sts. Bind off.

FINISHING: Sew shoulder seams. Run in yarn ends on wrong side.

Collar: From wrong side, sk first 4 sts at neck edge of left front. With double strand B and No. 10½ needles, pick up and k 13 sts on left front neck edge, pick up and k 7 sts on left back neck edge, k across sts on back holder, pick up and k 7 sts on right back neck edge, pick up and k 13 sts on right front neck edge, ending 4 sts in from center front edge—50 sts. Work in ribbing of k 1, p 1 for 1¼″. Change to No. 13 needles. Continue to work in ribbing until collar measures 8″ from start. Bind off loosely in ribbing.

Weave bound-off edge of sleeve to side armhole edge; sew bound-off underarm sts to side of sleeve. Sew side and sleeve seams.

From right side, with B and crochet hook, sl st across each front edge, being careful to keep work flat. Sew on buttons.

Drop-Shoulder Turtleneck

SIZES: Directions for small size (8–10). Changes for medium size (12–14) and large size (16–18) are in parentheses.

Body Bust Size: 31½″–32½″ (34″–36″; 38″–40″)

Finished Bust Size: 37½″ (41½″–47½″)

MATERIALS: Knitting worsted, 5 (6–6) 100-gram skeins. 14″ knitting needles, No. 9; 16″ circular needle, No. 9. Two stitch holders.

GAUGE: 13 sts = 5″ (pat).

PATTERN (multiple of 2 sts)

Note: To k 1 in row below next st, insert needle from front to back through hole below next st on needle, yarn around needle, draw through st; sl st above off left-hand needle. St will open up and lie across working strand.

Row 1: * P 1, k 1 in row below next st (see Note above), repeat from * across, end p 2. Repeat this row for pattern.

SWEATER BACK: Beg at lower edge with straight needles, cast on 48 (54–62) sts. Work in ribbing of k 1, p 1 for 2½″. Work in pat until piece measures 11½″ from start. Mark each side of last row for underarm. Work even until armholes measure 5½″ (5¾″–6″) above marked row.

Shape Neck: Keeping to pat as established, work 17 (20–23) sts, drop yarn, sl center 14 (14–16) sts on a holder; join another strand of yarn, finish row—17 (20–23) sts each side. Working on both sides at once, with separate strands of yarn, dec 1 st at beg of each neck edge 2 (2–3) times—15 (18–20) sts each side. Work even until armholes measure 7″ (7½″–8″) above marked row. Bind off in pat.

FRONT: Work same as for back.

SLEEVES: Beg at lower edge with straight needles, cast on 32 (32–34) sts. Work in ribbing of k 1, p 1 for 2″, inc 0 (2–2) sts across last row—32 (34–36) sts. Work in pat, inc 1 st each side every 2″ 4 times—40 (42–44) sts. Work even until piece measures 16½″ from start. Bind off in pat.

FINISHING: Sew shoulder seams.

Collar: Join yarn in right shoulder seam; from right side, with circular needle, pick up and k 10 sts on right back neck edge, k across sts on back holder, pick up and k 19 (20–19) sts on left neck edge, k across sts on front holder, pick up and k 9 (10–9) sts on right front neck edge—66 (68–70) sts. Join; work around in ribbing of k 1, p 1 for 7½″. Bind off loosely in ribbing.

With side edges of sleeves at underarm markers, bound-off edge at armhole edge, sew in sleeves. Sew side and sleeve seams.

Pastel-Pretty Winter Sweaters and Matching Accessories

This sweater and vest and the five accessories that match them—hats, scarves, mittens, socks, and bag—are knit in fresh hand-dyed springtime colors that will perk up any cold winter. Their hand-spun wool is luxuriantly soft and the crocheted picot-edging on some of the projects provides a lovely finishing touch.

SIZES: Directions for small size (8–10). Changes for medium size (12–14) and large size (16) are in parentheses.

Body Bust Size: 31½″–32½″ (34″–36″; 38″)

Blocked Bust Size: Sweater: 34″ (37″–41½″). **Vest:** 33½″ (36″–38″)

MATERIALS: Manos del Uruguay Handspun Hand-dyed Wool, 3.5 oz. skeins (see *Yarn Source Guide* at back of book or substitute knitting worsted using blue-gray in place of Butane Turquoise.): **Sweater:** 6 (7–7) skeins Cheek Pink (P), 1 skein each Blush (B), Butane Turquoise (T), English Green (G), White (W), and Parma Lavender (L). **Vest:** 4 skeins T; one skein each of B, G, and P. **Scarf and Socks:** 2 skeins P or T; for P background, 1 skein each of B, G, and W; for T background, 1 skein each of B, G, and P. **Hat, Gloves, and Bag:** 1 skein P or T; for P background, 1 skein each of B, G, T, and W; for T background, 1 skein each of B, G, and P.

For Sweater, Vest, and Hat: Knitting needles, Nos. 8 and 10 (5 mm and 6 mm). For Scarf: No. 10 needles. For Bag: No. 8 needles. For Gloves: Set of dp needles, No. 8 (9–10). For Socks: Set of dp needles, No. 10. For Sweater, Vest, and Scarf: Crochet hook, size G/6 (4¼ mm). Seven ⅝″ buttons for vest.

GAUGE: 15 sts = 4″; 17 rows = 4″ (Pat, No. 10 needles). 4 sts = 1″ (No. 9 needles). 17 sts = 4″ (No. 8 needles).

Pattern Notes: Always change colors on wrong side, picking up new strand from under dropped strand. Carry unused color across loosely; if more than 3 sts between colors, twist strands after every 3rd st. Cut and join colors when necessary.

Pastel Pullover

SWEATER FRONT: Beg at lower edge, with P and No. 8 needles, cast on 63 (71–79) sts. Work in ribbing of k 1, p 1, for 3″, inc 1 st each side of last row—65 (73–81) sts. Change to No. 10 needles. Working in stockinette st (k 1 row, p 1 row), work 2 rows Pink.

PATTERN

Row 1: Following Chart 1, k from D to F 8 (9–10) times, from F to G once.

Row 2: P from G to F once, from F to D 8 (9–10) times.

Rows 3–31: Working appropriate pat row, repeat last 2 rows to top of chart (31 rows), end k row.

Next Row: Following Chart 2, p from D to C once, from C to B 10 (11–12) times, from B to A once.

Next Row: K from A to B once, from B to C 10 (11–12) times, from C to D once. Working appropriate pat row, repeat these 2 rows to top of Chart 2 (14 rows), then repeat rows 9–14 once, rows 9–11 once, end p row.

Shape Neck: Working in pat as established (rows 9–14), beg with pat row 12, work 32 (36–40) sts, drop yarn, join another strand of color to be used, k 2 tog, finish row—32 (36–40) sts each side. Working on both sides at once, with separate strands of yarn, dec 1 st each neck edge every other row 9 (13–15) times, then every 4th row 2 (0–0) times; **at the same time,** when 25 (29–33) sts remain on each side, following Chart 3, work from right to center st on first side, from center st to right on 2nd side. Work to top of chart, then work with MC only until all decs are completed. Work even on remaining 21 (23–25) sts on each side until piece measures 6½″ (6¾″–7″) above first neck dec row.

Shape Shoulders: Bind off 7 (7–8) sts at beg of each arm side 3 (1–2) times, 0 (8–9) sts 0 (2–1) times.

BACK: Beg at lower edge, with P and No. 8 needles, cast on 65 (67–75) sts. Work in ribbing of k 1, p 1, for 3″. Change to No. 10 needles. Work in stockinette st until piece measures same as back to shoulder.

Shape Shoulders: Bind off 7 (7–8) sts at beg of next 6 (2–4) rows, 0 (8–9) sts next 0 (4–2) rows. Bind off remaining 23 (21–25) sts.

Sew shoulder seams. Mark back and front side edges 6″ (6½″–7½″) each side of shoulder seam for underarm.

Chart 1. Pullover, Vest, Scarf

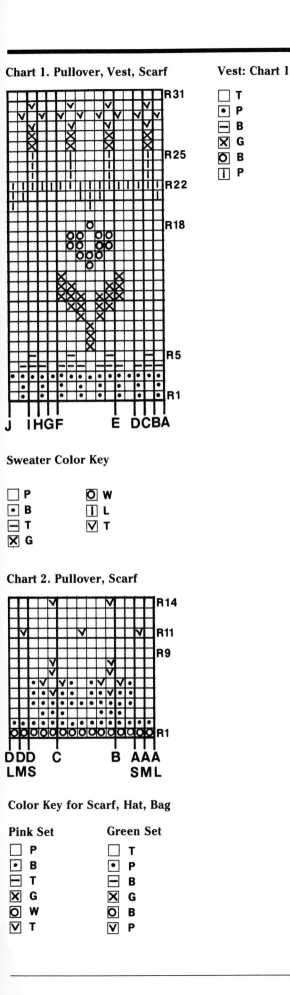

R31
R25
R22
R18
R5
R1

J IHGF E DCBA

Vest: Chart 1

☐	T
⊡	P
⊟	B
☒	G
⊙	B
⊡	P

Chart 3. Pullover

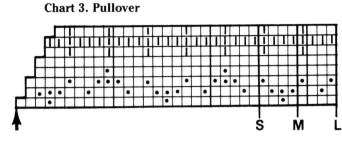

S   M   L

Chart 4. Hat, Bag

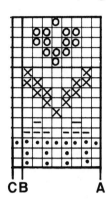

CB   A

Sweater Color Key

☐	P	⊙	W
⊡	B	⊡	L
⊟	T	☑	T
☒	G		

Chart 2. Pullover, Scarf

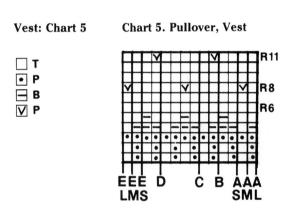

R14
R11
R9
R1

DDD C B AAA
LMS SML

Color Key for Scarf, Hat, Bag

Pink Set		Green Set	
☐	P	☐	T
⊡	B	⊡	P
⊟	T	⊟	B
☒	G	☒	G
⊙	W	⊙	B
☑	T	☑	P

Vest: Chart 5

☐	T
⊡	P
⊟	B
☑	P

Chart 5. Pullover, Vest

R11
R8
R6

EEE D C B AAA
LMS SML

SLEEVES: From right side, with P and No. 10 needles, beg at underarm marker, pick up and k 41 (49–51) sts on armhole edge, end at underarm marker.

PATTERN

Row 1 (wrong side): Following Chart 2, p from D to C once, from C to B 6 (7–7) times, from B to A once. Work in pat as established to top of chart (14 rows), then repeat rows 9–14 twice. Working with P only, dec 1 st each side of next row, then every 4" (2"–1½") 2 (6–6) times—35 (35–37) sts. Work even until piece measures 15½" from start or 2½" less than desired sleeve length. Change to No. 8 needles. Work in ribbing of k 1, p 1 for 2½".

Bind off loosely in ribbing. Work 2nd sleeve in same manner.

FINISHING: Run in yarn ends on wrong side. Sew side and sleeve seams.

Neckband

Rnd 1: Beg at shoulder seam, from right side, with crochet hook and P, sc around neck edge, being careful to keep work flat. Join with a sl st in first sc; do not turn.

Rnd 2: Ch 1, sc in back lp of each sc to 1 st before center front, (sk next sc, sc in back lp of next sc) twice, sc in back lp of each sc around. Join; do not turn.

Rnd 3 (picot rnd): Ch 1, sc in back lp of first sc, * ch 2, 2 sc in 2nd ch from hook (picot made), sk next 2 sc, sc in next sc, repeat from * around. Join; end off.

Steam-press lightly on wrong side.

Picot-edged Vest

VEST BACK Beg at lower edge, with T and No. 8 needles, cast on 57 (61–65) sts.

Ribbing

Row 1 (wrong side): P 1, * k 1, p 1, repeat from * across.

Row 2: K 1, * p 1, k 1, repeat from * across. Work in ribbing as established for 2½", end wrong side, inc 5 sts evenly spaced across last row—62 (66–70) sts. Change to No. 10 needles. Work in stockinette st (k 1 row, p 1 row) until piece measures 13½" from start. Mark each side of last row for underarm. Work even until armholes measure 7¼" (7½"–8") above marked row.

Shape Shoulders: Bind off 7 (8–8) sts at beg of next 6 (2–4) rows, 0 (7–7) sts next 0 (4–2) rows. Bind off remaining 20 (22–24) sts.

LEFT FRONT: Beg at lower edge, with T and No. 8 needles, cast on 31 (33–35) sts.

Row 1 (wrong side): K 6 (center band), p 1, * k 1, p 1, repeat from * across.

Row 2: K 1, * p 1, k 1, repeat from * to last 6 sts, end k 6 (center band). Repeat these 2

rows until piece measures 2½", end wrong side, inc 3 sts evenly spaced across ribbing on last row—34 (36–38) sts. Change to No. 10 needles. Working 6 sts (center band) with T in garter st throughout, remaining sts in stockinette st, work 2 rows, end wrong side.

PATTERN

Row 1: Following Chart 5, k from B to C 0 (1–0) times, from C to D 7 (7–8) times, k 6 T.

Row 2: K 6 T, p from D to C 7 (7–8) times, from C to B 0 (1–0) times.

Rows 3–7: Working appropriate pat row, repeat last 2 rows, end k row.

Row 8: K 6 T, p from E to D once, from D to B 3 times, from B to A once.

Row 9: K from A to B once, from B to D 3 times, from D to E once, k 6 T. Repeating last 2 rows, work to top of chart, then repeat rows 6–11 until piece measures same as back to underarm. Mark side edge of underarm. Work even until armhole measures 1¼" (1½"–2") above marked row, end p row.

YOKE PATTERN

Row 1: Following Chart 1, k from C (C–A) to D once, from D to F 3 times, from F to I (J–J) once, k 6 T.

Row 2: K 6 T, p from I (J–J) to F once, from F to D 3 times, from D to C (C–A) once. Work to end of row 25; **at the same time,** when armhole measures 4¼" (4½"–5") above marked row, bind off 10 sts at beg of center edge once, then dec 1 st at same edge every other row 3 (4–5) times—21 (22–23) sts. At end of row 25, work with T only until armhole measures same as back.

Shape Shoulder: Bind off 7 (8–8) sts at beg of arm side 3 (1–2) times, 0 (7–7) sts 0 (2–1) times.

With pins, mark position of 7 buttons, evenly spaced on left center band, first button 1" above lower edge, last button ½" below neck edge.

BUTTONHOLES: Beg at center edge, k 2, bind off next 2 sts, finish row.

Next Row: Cast on 2 sts over bound-off sts.

RIGHT FRONT: Cast on same as for left front.

Row 1 (wrong side): P 1, * k 1, p 1, repeat from * to last 6 sts, end k 6 (center band).

Row 2: K 6 (center band), * k 1, p 1, repeat from * across, end k 1. Work to correspond to left front, reversing pat and shaping, and working buttonholes opposite markers.

FINISHING: Run in yarn ends on wrong side. Sew side and shoulder seams.

Armhole Edging: From right side, join T in underarm seam.

Rnd 1: Sc around armhole edge. Join with a sl st in first sc; do not turn.

Rnd 2: * Sl st in each of next 2 sc, (dc, ch 3, sl st) in next st, repeat from * around. Join; end off.

Neck Edging

Row 1: Beg at right front neck edge, with T, sc around neck edge, end left front neck edge. End off.

Row 2: From right side, beg at right front edge, with T, work same as rnd 2 armhole edging around neck edge. End off.

Steam-press lightly on wrong side. Sew on buttons.

Scarf

Use P or T for main color (MC). With MC and No. 10 needles, cast on 33 sts.

Row 1: Knit.

Row 2: K 2 (border), p to last 2 sts, k 2 (border).

PATTERN

Row 1: K 2 MC; following Chart 1, k from B to D once, from D to F 3 times, from F to I once; with MC, k 2.

Row 2: K 2 MC; p from I to F once, from F to D 3 times, from D to B once; with MC, k 2.

Rows 3–18: Repeat last 2 rows to end of row 18.

Row 19: K 2 MC; following row 9 on Chart 2, k from small size A to B once, from B to C 4 times, from C to small size D once, k 2 MC.

Row 20: K 2 MC; following row 10, p from small size D to C once, from C to B 4 times, from B to small size A once; with MC, k 2. Working appropriate pat row, repeating last 2 rows, work to top of chart, then repeat rows 9–11. With MC, working first and last 2 sts in garter st, remaining sts in stockinette st, work even until piece measures 47″ from start or 6″ less than desired scarf length, end p row. Work pat in reverse to correspond to other end. Work last 2 rows with MC. Bind off.

Edging: From right side, join MC at left side edge at top of pattern. Being careful to keep work flat, sc to lower edge, 3 sc in corner, sc across lower edge, 3 sc in corner, sc on other side edge, end at top of pat. End off; do not turn.

Next Row: Join yarn in first sc; sl st in first sc, *(dc, ch 3, sc) in next sc, sl st in each of next 2 sc, repeat from * around, end sl st in last sc. End off. Work same edging on other end of scarf.

Hat

Note: Hat measures 19½″ around; will fit head size 22″. For larger size, use No. 10½ needles. Beg at lower edge, with MC (use P or T for MC) and No. 8 needles, cast on 71 sts loosely. Work in ribbing of k 1, p 1 for 5″, inc 1 st each side of last row—73 sts. Change to No. 10 needles. Work in stockinette st for 4 rows, end p row.

PATTERN

Row 1: Following Chart 4, k from A to B to last st, end k from B to C once.

Row 2: P from C to B once, from B to A across. Working appropriate pat row, repeat last 2 rows to top of chart (row 15), end k row. With MC, p 1 row, dec 1 st each side—71 sts.

Shape Top

Row 1: K 2 MC, k 1 CC (use T or P), * with MC, k 1, k 3 tog, k 1, k 1 CC, k 3 MC, k 1 CC, repeat from * 5 times, end with MC, k 1, k 3 tog, k 1, k 1 CC, k 2 MC—57 sts. With MC, work 3 rows.

Row 5: With MC, k 3, k 3 tog, k 2, k 1 CC, *with MC, k 2, k 3 tog, k 2; k 1 CC, repeat from * 5 times—43 sts. With MC, work 3 rows.

Row 9: With MC, k 2, *k 3 tog, k 3, repeat from * across, end last repeat k 2—29 sts.

Row 10: Purl.

Row 11: K 1, * k 3 tog, k 2, repeat from * across, end last repeat k 1—15 sts.

Row 12: Purl. Cut MC.

Row 13: With CC, k 1, (k 2 tog) 7 times—8 sts. Cut yarn, leaving a long end for sewing. Thread needle; draw sts tog tightly. Fasten securely on wrong side; weave back seam. Fold cuff to right side.

Bag

Work same as for hat for 2″.

Next Row (eyelet row): K 1, * yo, k 2 tog, p 1, yo, k 2 tog, k 1, repeat from * across.

Next Row: Work in ribbing across. Complete same as for hat; do not change to larger needles. Work entire bag with No. 8 needles.

DRAWSTRINGS (make 2): Cut a 5-yard strand of MC; fold in half and make twisted cord as shown at end of instructions. Weave one end of drawstring through eyelets. Beg at opposite side of bag, draw 2nd drawstring through eyelets. With R and P, make two pompoms; attach to end of drawstrings on each side of bag.

Gloves

Fits size 7. Changes for sizes 7½ and 8 are in parentheses.

RIGHT GLOVE: With No. 8 (9–10) dp needles and MC (use P or T for MC), cast on 33 sts. Do not join; work back and forth in ribbing of k 1, p 1 for 2½″. Working in stockinette st, k 1 row.

PATTERN

Row 1: Following Chart 6, p from C to B once, from B to A 4 times.

Row 2: K from A to B 4 times, from B to C once.

Rows 3–5: Working appropriate pat row, work to end of row 5, end p row.

Shape Thumb

Next Row: K 8 MC, k 1 G for start of flower on back of glove, k 6 MC, put and keep a marker on needle, inc 1 st (to inc 1 st, k in strand between sts), k 3, inc 1 st, put a marker on needle, k 15—35 sts. Following Chart 6 for flower pat as established, work remaining sts with MC, inc 1 st after first marker and before 2nd marker every row 3 times more—41 sts.

Next Row: P 15, sl next 11 sts on a holder, p 15, working flower pat as established—30 sts. Work to top of chart (row 15), end p row.

Next Row: K 4 MC, k 1 CC, k 5 MC, k 1 CC, k 19 MC. With MC, purl 1 row.

Next Row: K 1 MC, k 1 CC, k 5 MC, k 1 CC, k 22 MC. With MC, work even until piece measures 7″ from start or desired length to base of fingers, end p row. Cut MC; sl first 11 sts to holder for back of hand, sl last 11 sts to another holder for palm—8 sts remain on needle.

First Finger: Divide the 8 sts on 3 dp needles. Join; with MC, work around in stockinette st (k each rnd) until finger measures 2¼″ (2½″–3″) from base or ⅜″ less than desired length. Cut MC; join CC. With CC, k 2 rnds. Cut yarn, leaving an 8″ length. Thread needle, draw through sts and fasten securely on wrong side.

2nd Finger: From right side, with MC and dp needle, k 4 from back holder, pick up and k 1 st in base of first finger, k 4 from palm, cast on 1 st—10 sts. Divide sts on 3 dp needles. Join; work around in stockinette st until piece measures 2½″ (2¾″–3″) from base.

Cut MC; join CC. With CC, k 2 rnds. Complete same as first finger.

3rd Finger: From right side, with MC and dp needle, k 4 from back holder, pick up and k 1 st in base of 2nd finger, k 4 from palm, cast on 1 st—10 sts. Divide sts on 3 dp needles. Join; work same as for first finger.

4th Finger: From right side, with MC and dp needle, k 3 from back holder, pick up and k 1 st in base of 3rd finger, k 3 from palm—7 sts. Divide sts on 3 dp needles. Join; work same as for first finger until piece measures 1½″ (1¾″–2″) from base. Cut MC; join CC. With CC, k 2 rnds. Complete same as first finger.

Thumb: Sl the 11 sts from holder to 3 dp needles. With MC, work in stockinette st until thumb measures 1½″ (1¾″–2″) from start. Cut MC; join CC. With CC, k 2 rnds. Complete same as first finger.

LEFT GLOVE: Work same as right glove to start of thumb.

Next Row: K 15 MC, put a marker on needle, inc 1 st, k 3, inc 1 st, put a marker on needle, k 6, k 1 G for start of flower, k 8 MC. Complete same as for right glove, reversing palm and back of hand.

Socks

With MC and No. 8 needles, cast on loosely 43 sts. Do not join; work back and forth in ribbing of k 1, p 1 for 3″. Change to No. 10 needles. Work in stockinette st (k 1 row, p 1 row) until piece measures 6″ from start, end p row.

PATTERN

Row 1: K 3 MC, k 1 CC, (k 5 MC, k 1 CC) 6 times, k 3 MC. With MC, work 2 rows.

Row 4: P 6 MC, p 1 CC, (p 5 MC, p 1 CC) 5 times, p 6 MC. With MC, work 2 rows.

Row 7: Repeat row 1.

Row 8: Following row 18 on Chart 7, p from H to D once, from F to D 4 times, from D to C once.

Row 9: Working row 17, k from C to D once, from D to F 4 times, from D to H once. Repeating last 2 rows, working chart in reverse, work to row 1, end p row. Divide sts on 3 dp needles. Join; mark beg of rnd.

Next Rnd (dec rnd): From right side, k 1, k 2 tog, k to last 3 sts, sl 1, k 1, psso, k 1—2 sts dec. Work around in stockinette st (k each rnd), repeat dec rnd every 6th rnd 4 times more—33 sts. Work even until piece measures 18″ from start or desired length from top of heel (cuff will be turned to right side), dec 1 st at end of last row—32 sts.

Heel: K 8, sl next 16 sts on a holder, sl remaining 8 sts on heel needle—16 sts. Turn.

Next Row: Sl 1, p 15.

Next Row: Sl 1, k 15. Repeat these 2 rows 3 times.

Chart 6: Gloves

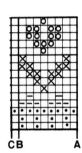

CB   A

Color Key for Gloves, Socks

Pink set

□ P	☒ G
· B	◉ W
⊟ T	☑ T

Green set

□ T	☒ G
· P	◉ B
⊟ B	☑ P

Chart 7: Socks

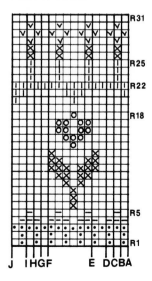

J IHGF   E DCBA

Turn Heel: Sl 1, p 8, p 2 tog, p 1, turn; sl 1, k 3, sl 1, k 1, psso, k 1, turn; sl 1, p 4, p 2 tog, p 1, turn; sl 1, k 5, sl 1, k 1, psso, k 1, turn; sl 1, p 6, p 2 tog, p 1, turn; sl 1, k 7, sl 1, k 1, psso, k 1—10 sts.

Shape Instep: Pick up and k 8 sts on side of heel; with 2nd dp needle, k 16 from holder; with 3rd dp needle, pick up and k 8 sts on side of heel, k 5 from heel needle—13 sts on first and 3rd dp needles, 16 sts on 2nd dp needle. Mark beg of rnd.

Shape Gussets

Rnd 1: Knit.

Rnd 2: K to last 3 sts on first needle, k 2 tog, k 1; on 2nd needle, k 16; on 3rd needle, k 1, sl 1, k 1, psso, k to end of rnd—2 sts dec. Repeat last 2 rnds 4 times—32 sts. K around until foot measures 2″ less than desired length to tip of toe.

Shape Toe

Rnd 1: K to last 3 sts on first dp needle, k 2 tog, k 1; on 2nd dp needle, k 1, sl 1, k 1, psso, k to last 3 sts, k 2 tog, k 1; on 3rd dp needle, k 1, sl 1, k 1, psso, k to end—4 sts dec. K 1 rnd. Repeat last 2 rnds 3 times—16 sts. With 3rd dp needle, k sts from first needle. Cut yarn, leaving a long end. Weave toe tog with Kitchener st (see directions following). Make second sock in same manner.

FINISHING: Run in yarn ends on wrong side. Sew back seam; weave cuff on right side. Steam socks lightly on wrong side. Fold cuff to right side.

MAKING A TWISTED CORD: This method requires two people. Tie one end of yarn around pencil. Loop yarn over center of second pencil, back to and around first, back to second, making as many strands between pencils as needed for thickness of cord; knot

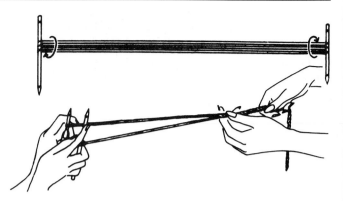

end to pencil. Length of yarn between pencils should be three times desired cord length. Each person holds yarn just below pencil with one hand, twists pencil with other hand, keeping yarn taut. When yarn begins to kink, catch center over doorknob or hook. Bring pencils together for one person to hold, while other grasps center of yarn, sliding hand down at short intervals and letting yarn twist.

WEAVING WITH KITCHENER STITCH: Divide stitches evenly on two needles and hold parallel, with yarn end coming from first stitch on back needle. Break off yarn, leaving about 12″ end on work. Thread this end into a tapestry needle. Working from right to left, * pass needle through first stitch on front needle as if to knit and slip stitch off needle, pass yarn through 2nd stitch on front needle as if to purl but leave stitch on needle, pass yarn through first stitch on back needle as if to purl and slip stitch off needle; pass yarn through 2nd stitch on back needle as if to knit, but leave on needle. Repeat from * until all stitches are woven.

"Zippy" Aran Sweaters for the Whole Family

These practical zippered variations on the traditional Aran Sweater include a reversible zippered vest. Matching hats top them off.

Adult Aran Vest

SIZES: Directions are for small size (36–38). Changes for medium size (40–42) and large size (44) are in parentheses.

Body Chest Size: 36"–38" (40"–42"; 44")

Blocked Chest Size (closed): 42½" (44½"–46½")

MATERIALS: Emu Aran (from Merino Wool Co. See *Yarn Source Guide* at back of book.), 8 (9–10) 50-gram balls. (**Note:** Emu Aran is 100% wool.) Knitting needles, No. 10. One dp needle for cable. One yard 54"-wide woolen fabric for lining. Matching sewing thread. Reversible separating zipper.

GAUGE: 4 sts = 1".

PATTERN NOTES

Note 1: Sl all sl sts as if to purl.

Note 2: Right Cross st (rc st): K in front of 2nd st, k in front of first st, sl both sts off left-hand needle.

Note 3: Left Twist St (lt st): With dp needle, sl next 2 sts and hold in front of work, p next st, then k 2 sts from dp needle.

Note 4: Right Twist St (rt st): With dp needle, sl next st and hold in back of work, k next 2 sts, then p st from dp needle.

Note 5: Popcorn: K, p, k in next st or horizontal bar (see Pattern), turn; p 3, turn; k 3 tog (1 st of group left).

PATTERN STITCHES

PATTERN 1 (worked on an even number of sts)

Row 1 (right side): Purl.

Row 2: * K 1, p 1, repeat from * across. Repeat these 2 rows for pat 1.

PATTERN 2 (worked on 3 sts)

Row 1 (right side): Knit.

Row 2: Purl.

Row 3: With dp needle, sl next 2 sts and hold in back of work, k 1, then k 2 from dp needle.

Row 4: Purl. Repeat these 4 rows for pat 2.

PATTERN 3 (worked on 14 sts)

Row 1 (right side): P 5; with dp needle, sl next 2 sts and hold in front of work, k next 2 sts, then k 2 from dp needle, p 5.

Rows 2, 4, 6, 8 and 10: K all k sts, p all p sts.

Row 3: P 4, rt st (see Note 4) on next 3 sts, lt st (see Note 3) on next 3 sts, p 4.

Row 5: P 3, rt st on next 3 sts, p 2, lt st on next 3 sts, p 3.

Row 7: P 2, rt st on next 3 sts, p 2; work popcorn in horizontal strand between sts (see Note 5), p 2, lt st on next 3 sts, p 2.

Note: There will be 1 st more on rows 7–11.

Row 9: P 1, rt st on next 3 sts, p 2, popcorn in next st, p 1, popcorn in next st, p 2, lt st on next 3 sts, p 1.

Row 11: P 1, lt st on next 3 sts, p 3, popcorn in next st, p 3, rt st on next 3 sts, p 1.

Row 12: K 2, p 2, k 2, k 2 tog, k 3, p 2, k 2.

Row 13: P 2, lt st on next 3 sts, p 4, rt st on next 3 sts, p 2.

Rows 14 and 16: Repeat row 2.

Row 15: P 3, lt st on next 3 sts, p 2, rt st on next 3 sts, p 3.

Row 17: P 4, lt st on next 3 sts, rt st on next 3 sts, p 4.

Row 18: Repeat row 3. Repeat rows 1–18 for pat 3.

Adult Vest

VEST BACK: Beg at lower edge, cast on 80 (84–88) sts.

PATTERN

Row 1 (right side): Work first 22 (24–26) sts in pat 1, p 2, rc st (see Note 2) on next 2 sts, p 1; work next 3 sts in pat 2, p 1, rc st on next 2 sts; work next 14 sts in pat 3, rc st on next 2 sts, p 1, work next 3 sts in pat 2, p 1, rc st on next 2 sts, p 2; work last 22 (24–26) sts in pat 1.

Row 2: Working appropriate pat row, work first 22 (24–26) sts in pat 1, k 2, p 2, k 1; work next 3 sts in pat 2, k 1, p 2; work next 14 sts in pat 3, p 2, k 1; work next 3 sts in pat 2, k 1, p 2, k 2; work last 22 (24–26) sts in pat 1. Working appropriate pat row, repeat last 2 rows until piece measures 17″ (18″–18″) from start or desired length to underarm, end wrong side. Piece should measure 20″ (21″–22″) wide.

Shape Armholes: Keeping to pat as established, bind off 5 sts at beg of next 2 rows. Dec 1 st each side every other row 3 times—64 (68–72) sts. Work even until armholes measure 8″ (8½″–9″) above first bound-off sts.

Shape Shoulders: Bind off 7 sts at beg of next 6 rows, 7 (8–9) sts next 2 rows. Bind off remaining 8 (10–12) sts loosely.

RIGHT FRONT: Beg at lower edge, cast on 45 (47–49) sts.

PATTERN

Row 1 (right side): K 5 (center band), rc st on next 2 sts, p 1; work next 3 sts in pat 2, p 1, rc st on next 2 sts; work next 14 sts in pat 3, rc st on next 2 sts, p 1; work next 3 sts in pat 2, p 1, rc st on next sts, p 2, work last 6 (8–10) sts in pat 1.

Row 2: Work first 6 (8–10) sts in pat 1, k 2, p 2, k 1; work next 3 sts in pat 2, k 1, p 2; work next 14 sts in pat 3, p 2, k 1; work next 3 sts in pat 2, k 1, p 2, k 5 (center band). Working appropriate pat row, repeat last 2 rows until piece measures same as back to underarm, end side edge. Piece should measure 11¼" (11¾"–12¼") wide.

Shape Armhole: Keeping to pat as established, bind off 5 sts at beg of side edge once. Dec 1 st at same edge every other row 3 times—37 (39–41) sts. Work even until armhole measures 5" (5½"–6") above bound-off sts, end center edge.

Shape Neck And Shoulder: Bind off 6 sts at beg of center edge once. Dec 1 st at beg of same edge 3 (4–5) times—28 (29–30) sts. Work even until armhole measures same as back. Bind off 7 sts at beg of arm side 3 times, 7 (8–9) sts once.

LEFT FRONT: Cast on same as for right front.

PATTERN

Row 1 (right side): Work first 6 (8–10) sts in pat 1, p 2, rc st on next 2 sts, p 1; work next 3 sts in pat 2, p 1, rc st on next 2 sts; work next 14 sts in pat 3, rc st on next 2 sts, p 1; work next 3 sts in pat 2, p 1, rc st on next 2 sts, k 5 (center band).

Row 2: K 5 (center band), p 2, k 1; work next 3 sts in pat 2, k 1, p 2; work next 14 sts in pat 3, p 2, k 1; work next 3 sts in pat 2, k 1, p 2, k 2; work next 6 (8–10) sts in pat 1. Working appropriate pat row, repeating last 2 rows,

complete same as for right front, reversing shaping.

FINISHING: Block pieces. Using knitted pieces for pat, cut lining fabric to fit back and fronts, allowing ½" on all edges. Stitch shoulder and side seams of lining. Sew shoulder and side seams of knitted pieces. Pin lining to wrong side of vest. Sew outer edges of vest and lining tog, leaving center fronts open. Insert zipper between lining and vest; sew in place.

LOWER BAND: Cast on 9 sts.

Row 1 (right side): Knit.

Row 2: K 4, p 1 for fold line, k 4. Repeat these 2 rows until piece, when slightly stretched, measures same as lower edge of vest. Bind off. Make two armbands and one neckband in same manner.

Fold bands in half on turning st. With edge of vest at fold, hem each band in place. Steam-press lightly.

Child's Aran Vest

SIZE: Directions are for size 6. Changes for sizes 8 and 10 are in parentheses.

Body Chest Size: 24" (26"–28")

Blocked Chest Size (closed): 32" (34"–36")

MATERIALS: Emu Aran (from Merino Wool Co. See *Yarn Source Guide* at back of book.), 4 (4–5) 50-gram balls for vest, 1 for hat. (**Note:** Emu Aran is 100% wool.) Knitting needles No. 10. One dp needle for cable. ½ (¾–¾) yard 54"-wide woolen fabric for lining. Matching sewing thread. Reversible separating zipper.

GAUGE: 4 sts = 1".

Note: Pattern notes and pattern stitches same as for Adult Vest.

VEST BACK: Beg at lower edge, cast on 60 (64–68) sts.

PATTERN

Row 1 (right side): P 14 (16–18), rc st (see Note 2) on next 2 sts, p 1; work next 3 sts in pat 2, p 1, rc st on next 2 sts; work next 14 sts in pat 3, rc st on next 2 sts, p 1; work next 3 sts in pat 2, p 1, rc st on next 2 sts, p 14 (16–18).

Row 2: K 14 (16–18), k 2, p 1; working appropriate pat row, work next 3 sts in pat 2, k 1, p 2; work next 14 sts in pat 3, p 2, k 1; work next 3 sts in pat 2, k 1, p 2, k 14 (16–18). Working appropriate pat row, repeat last 2 rows until piece measures 9″ (9½″–9½″) from start or desired length to underarm, end wrong side. Piece should measure 15″ (16″–17″) wide.

Shape Armholes: Keeping to pat as established, bind off 3 (4–4) sts at beg of next 2 rows. Dec 1 st each side every other row 3 (3–4) times—48 (50–52) sts. Work even until armholes measure 5″ (5½″–6″) above first bound-off sts.

Shape Shoulders: Bind off 5 sts at beg of next 8 rows. Bind off loosely remaining 8 (10–12) sts.

RIGHT FRONT: Beg at lower edge, cast on 35 (37–39) sts.

PATTERN

Row 1 (right side): K 5 (center band), rc st on next 2 sts, p 1; work next 3 sts in pat 2, p 1, rc st on next 2 sts; work next 14 sts in pat 3, rc st on next 2 sts, p 1; work next 3 sts in pat 2, p 1 (3–5).

Row 2: K 1 (3–5); work next 3 sts in pat 2, k 1, p 2; work next 14 sts in pat 3, p 2, k 1; work next 3 sts in pat 2, k 1, p 2, k 5 (center band). Working appropriate pat row, repeat last 2 rows until piece measures same as back to underarm, end side edge. Piece should measure 8¾″ (9¼″–9¾″) wide.

Shape Armhole: Keeping to pat as established, bind off 3 (4–4) sts at beg of side edge once. Dec 1 st at same edge every other row 3 (3–4) times—29 (30–31) sts. Work even until armhole measures 3½″ (3¾″–4″) above bound-off sts, end center edge.

Shape Neck and Shoulder: Bind off 4 sts at beg of center edge once. Dec 1 st at same edge every other row 5 (6–7) times; **at the**

same time, when armhole measures same as back, bind off 5 sts at beg of arm side 4 times.

LEFT FRONT: Cast on same as for right front.

PATTERN

Row 1 (right side): P 1 (3–5); work next 3 sts in pat 2, p 1, rc st on next 2 sts; work next 14 sts in pat 3, rc st on next 2 sts, p 1; work next 3 sts in pat 2, p 1; rc st on next 2 sts, k 5 (center band).

Row 2: K 5 (center band), p 2, k 1; work next 3 sts in pat 2, k 1, p 2; work next 14 sts in pat 3, p 2, k 1; work next 3 sts in pat 2, k 1 (3–5). Working appropriate pat row, repeating last 2 rows, complete same as for right front, reversing shaping.

FINISHING: Complete same as for adult aran vest.

Child's Aran Hat

Beg at lower edge, cast on 70 sts.

Row 1 (wrong side): K 1, * p 2, k 1, repeat from * across.

Row 2: P 1, * rc st on next 2 sts, p 1, repeat from * across.

Rows 3–5: Repeat rows 1, 2, 1, inc 2 sts evenly spaced across last row—72 sts.

PATTERN:

Row 1 (right side): * P 3, rc st on next 2 sts, p 1; work next 3 sts in pat 2, p 1, rc st on next 2 sts; work next 14 sts in pat 3, rc st on next 2 sts, p 1; work next 3 sts in pat 2, p 1, rc st on next 2 sts, p 1, repeat from * once.

Row 2: * K 1, p 2, k 1; following appropriate pat row, work next 3 sts in pat 2, k 1, p 2; work next 14 sts in pat 3, p 2, k 1; work next 3 sts in pat 2, k 1, p 2, k 3, repeat from * once. Working appropriate pat row, repeat last 2 rows to end of row 18 of pat 3, then repeat pat rows 1 and 2 of pat 3, end wrong side.

Shape Top:

Next Row (right side): (P 6, p 2 tog) 9 times, K 1 row.

Next Row: (P 5, p 2 tog) 9 times. K 1 row.

Next Row: (P 4, p 2 tog) 9 times. K 1 row.

Next Row: (P 3, p 2 tog) 9 times. K 1 row.

Next Row: (P 2, p 2 tog) 9 times. K 1 row.

Next Row: (P 1, p 2 tog) 9 times. K 2 tog across—9 sts. Cut yarn, leaving a long end. Draw sts tog; fasten securely on wrong side.

Sew back seam. Steam-press lightly. Make pompon; attach to top of hat.

Adult Aran Jacket

SIZES: Directions for small size (8–10). Any changes for medium size (12–14) and large size (16) are in parentheses.

Note: All sizes are made the same. Needle size and gauge determine size.

Body Bust Size: 31½″–32½″ (34″–36″; 38″)

Blocked Bust Size (closed): 38″ (42½″–47¾″)

MATERIALS: Emu Aran (from Merino Wool Co. See *Yarn Source Guide* at back of book.), 13 (13–14) 50-gram balls. (**Note:** Emu Aran is 100% wool.) Knitting needles No. 8 (9–10). One dp needle. Separating zipper. 1½ yards 54″-wide wool fabric for lining. Matching sewing thread.

GAUGE: 5 sts = 1″ (No. 8 needles). 9 sts = 2″ (No. 9 needles). 4 sts = 1″ (No. 10 needles).

Note 1: Sl all sl sts as if to p.

Note 2: Right Cross St (rc st): K 2nd st, k first st, sl both sts off left-hand needle.

Note 3: Left Twist St (lt st): With dp needle, sl next 2 sts and hold in front of work, p next st, then k 2 sts from dp needle.

Note 4: Right Twist St (rt st): With dp needle, sl next st and hold in back of work, k next 2 sts, then p st from dp needle.

PATTERN STITCHES

PATTERN 1 (worked on 3 sts)

Row 1 (right side): Knit.

Row 2: Purl.

Row 3: With dp needle, sl next 2 sts and hold in back of work, k 1, then k 2 from dp needle.

Row 4: Purl. Repeat these 4 rows for pat 1.

PATTERN 2 (worked on 6 sts)

Row 1 (right side): Knit.

Row 2: Purl.

Row 3: With dp needle, sl next 2 sts and hold in back of work, k 1, then k 2 from dp needle; with dp needle, sl next st, hold in front of work, k 2, then k 1 from dp needle.

Row 4: Purl. Repeat these 4 rows for pat 2.

PATTERN 3 (worked on 16 sts)

Row 1 (right side): P 1, lt st (see Note 3) on next 3 sts, p 8, rt st (see Note 4) on next 3 sts, p 1.

Row 2 And All Even Rows: K all k sts, p all p sts.

Row 3: P 2, lt st on next 3 sts, p 6, rt st on next 3 sts, p 2.

Row 5: P 3, lt st on next 3 sts, p 4, rt st on next 3 sts, p 3.

Row 7: P 4, lt st on next 3 sts, p 2, rt st on next 3 sts, p 4.

Row 9: P 5, lt st on next 3 sts, rt st on next 3 sts, p 5.

Row 11: P 6; with dp needle, sl next 2 sts and hold in front of work, k 2, then k 2 from dp needle, p 6.

Row 13: P 5; with dp needle, sl next st and hold in back of work, k 2, then p 1 from dp needle; with dp needle, sl next 2 sts and hold in front of work, p 1, then k 2 from dp needle, p 5.

Row 15: Repeat row 9.

Row 17: Repeat row 11.

Row 19: Repeat row 13.

Row 21: P 4, rt st on next 3 sts, p 2, lt st on next 3 sts, p 4.

Row 23: P 3, rt st on next 3 sts, p 4, lt st on next 3 sts, p 3.

Row 25: P 2, rt st on next 3 sts, p 6, lt st on next 3 sts, p 2.

Row 27: P 1, rt st on next 3 sts, p 8, lt st on next 3 sts, p 1.

Row 28: Repeat row 2. Repeat these 28 rows for pat 3.

JACKET BACK: Beg at lower edge, cast on 93 sts.

PATTERN

Row 1 (right side): P 3, rc st (see Note 2) on next 2 sts, p 1; work next 3 sts in pat 1, p 1, rc st on next 2 sts, p 3; work next 6 sts in pat 2, p 3, rc st on next 2 sts; work next 16 sts in pat 3, rc st on next 2 sts, p 1; work next 3 sts in pat 1, p 1, rc st on next 2 sts; work next 16 sts in pat 3, rc st on next 2 sts, p 3, work next 6 sts in pat 2, p 3, rc st on next 2 sts, p 1; work pat 1 on next 3 sts, p 1, rc st on next 2 sts, p 3.

Row 2: K 1, p 1, k 1, p 2, k 1; working appropriate pat row, work next 3 sts in pat 1, k 1, p 2, k 3; work next 6 sts in pat 2, k 3, p 2; work next 16 sts in pat 3, p 2, k 1; work next 3 sts in pat 1, k 1, p 2; work next 16 sts in pat 3, p 2, k 3; work next 6 sts in pat 2, k 3, p 2, k 1; work pat 1 on next 3 sts, k 1, p 2, k 1, p 1, k 1.

Repeating last 2 rows, working appropriate pat row, work in pat as established until piece measures 15″ from start or desired length to underarm. Piece should measure 18½″ (20¾″–23¼″) wide.

Shape Armholes: Keeping to pat as established, bind off 9 sts at beg of next 2 rows—75 sts. Work even until armholes measure 7″ (7½″–8″) above first bound-off sts.

Shape Shoulders: Bind off 7 sts at beg of next 8 rows. Bind off remaining 19 sts.

RIGHT FRONT: Beg at lower edge, cast on 49 sts.

PATTERN

Row 1 (right side): K 5 (center band), rc st on next 2 sts; work next 16 sts in pat 3, rc st on next 2 sts, p 3, work next 6 sts in pat 2, p 3, rc st on next 2 sts, p 1, work next 3 sts in pat 1, p 1, rc st on next 2 sts, p 3.

Row 2: K 1, p 1, k 1, p 2, k 1; working appropriate row, work next 3 sts in pat 1, k 1, p 2, k 3; work next 6 sts in pat 2, k 3, p 2; work next 16 sts in pat 3, p 2, k 5 (center band).

Repeating last 2 rows, working appropriate pat row, work in pat as established until piece measures same as back to underarm, end side edge. Piece should measure 9¾″ (11″–12¼″) wide.

Shape Armhole: Keeping to pat, bind off 9 sts at beg of side edge once—40 sts. Work even until armhole measures 5″ (5½″–6″) above bound-off sts, end center edge.

Shape Neck and Shoulder: Bind off 7 sts at beg of center edge once, then dec 1 st at same edge every row 5 times; **at the same time,** when armhole measures same as back, bind off 7 sts at beg of arm side 4 times.

LEFT FRONT: Cast on same as for right front.

PATTERN

Row 1 (right side): P 3, rc st on next 2 sts, p 1; work next 3 sts in pat 1, p 1, rc st on next 2 sts, p 3; work next 6 sts in pat 2, p 3, rc st on next 2 sts; work next 16 sts in pat 3, rc st on next 2 sts, k 5 (center band).

Row 2: K 5 (center band), p 2; work next 16 sts in pat 3, p 2, k 3; work next 6 sts in pat 2, k 3, p 2, k 1; work next 3 sts in pat 1, k 1, p 2, k 1, p 1, k 1.

Working appropriate pat row, repeating last 2 rows, complete as for right front, reversing shaping.

SLEEVES: Beg at lower edge, cast on 50 sts.

PATTERN

Row 1 (right side): P 19, rc st on next 2 sts, p 1; work next 6 sts in pat 2, p 1, rc st on next 2 sts, p 19.

Row 2: K 19, p 2, k 1; working appropriate pat row, work next 6 sts in pat 2, k 1, p 2, k 19. Repeat last 2 rows, inc 1 st each side every 3″ 4 times, working added sts into reverse stockinette st (p on right side, k on wrong side)—58 sts. Work even until piece measures 18″ (18½″–19″) from start or desired sleeve length. Bind off.

RIGHT POCKET: Beg at lower edge, cast on 27 sts.

PATTERN

Row 1 (right side:) P 1, rc st on next 2 sts, p 3; work next 6 sts in pat 2, p 3, rc st on next 2 sts, p 1; work next 3 sts in pat 1, p 1, rc st on next 2 sts, p 3.

Row 2: K 1, p 1, k 1, p 2, k 1; work next 3 sts in pat 1, k 1, p 2, k 3; work next 6 sts in pat 2, k 3, p 2, k 1. Repeat last 2 rows until piece measures 8″ from start, end right side. Bind off loosely in pat.

LEFT POCKET: Cast on same as for right pocket.

PATTERN

Row 1 (right side): P 3, rc st on next 2 sts, p 1; work next 3 sts in pat 1, p 1, rc st on next 2 sts, p 3; work next 6 sts in pat 2, p 3, rc st on next 2 sts, p 1.

Row 2: K 1, p 2, k 3; work next 6 sts in pat 2, k 3, p 2, k 1; work next 3 sts in pat 1, k 1, p 2, k 1, p 1, k 1. Complete same as for right pocket.

FINISHING: Block pieces. Using knitted pieces for pat, cut fabric to fit back, fronts and sleeves, allowing ½″ on all edges. Stitch shoulder seams, sew in sleeves, sew side and sleeve seams of lining. Sew shoulder seams, sew in sleeves, sew side and sleeve seams of knitted pieces. Pin lining to wrong side of jacket. Sew outer edge of jacket and lining tog, leaving center fronts open. Sew zipper between lining and jacket. Cut fabric ½″ larger than pockets; hem lining to pockets.

LOWER BAND: Cast on 9 sts.

Row 1 (right side): Knit.

Row 2: K 4, p 1 for turning st, k 4. Repeat these 2 rows until piece, when slightly stretched, measures same as lower edge of jacket. Bind off.

SLEEVE BANDS (make 2): Work same as for lower band until piece, when slightly stretched, measures same as lower edge of sleeve. Bind off.

NECKBAND: Cast on 90 sts. Work in ribbing of k 1, p 1 for 1½″. P next row on right side for turning ridge. Work in ribbing of k 1, p 1 for 1½″. Bind off loosely in ribbing.

INNER WRISTBANDS (make 2): Beg at lower edge, cast on 48 sts. Work in ribbing of k 1, p 1 for 4″. Bind off loosely in ribbing.

Fold lower band and sleeve bands in half at turning st. With edge of jacket at turning ridge, hem each side of bands to lower edge of jacket and sleeves. Fold collar in half on turning ridge; with neck edge of jacket at fold, hem each side of neckband to jacket.

Weave edges of wristband tog, forming tube. With lower edge of wristband 1″ above lower edge of sleeve, hem upper edge of wristband to lining. Sew pockets in place with lower edge of pocket at top edge of band, matching patterns of fronts.

Adult Aran Hat

SIZE: Medium.

MATERIALS: Emu Aran (from Merino Wool Co. See *Yarn Source Guide* at back of book.), 1 50-gram ball. Knitting needles No. 10. One dp needle. Lining fabric. Matching sewing thread.

GAUGE: 4 sts = 1″.

Note: Sl all sl sts as if to p.

HAT SECTIONS (make 5): Beg at lower edge, cast on 19 sts.

PATTERN

Row 1 (right side): P 5; with dp needle, sl next st and hold in back of work, k 1, then k st from dp needle (right cross st, rc st, made), p 1, k 3, p 1, rc st on next 2 sts, p 5.

Row 2: K 5, p 2, k 1, p 3, k 1, p 2, k 5.

Row 3: P 5, rc st on next 2 sts, p 1; with dp needle, sl next 2 sts and hold in back of work, k next st, then k 2 from dp needle, p 1, rc st on next 2 sts, p 5.

Row 4: Repeat row 2. Repeat rows 1–4 for pat until piece measures 3″ from start.

Shape Top: Keeping to pat as established, dec 1 st each side every other row 8 times—3 sts remain. K 3 tog; end off.

BAND: Cast on 12 sts. Work in garter st (k each row) until piece, when slightly stretched, measures 23″. Bind off.

FINISHING: Using pattern, cut 5 lining sections; sew seams. Block pieces. Weave sections tog. Insert lining in hat; sew lower edge of hat to lining. Weave cast-on edge of band to bound-off edge, forming circle. Fold band in half over lower edge of hat; hem both sides of band to hat.

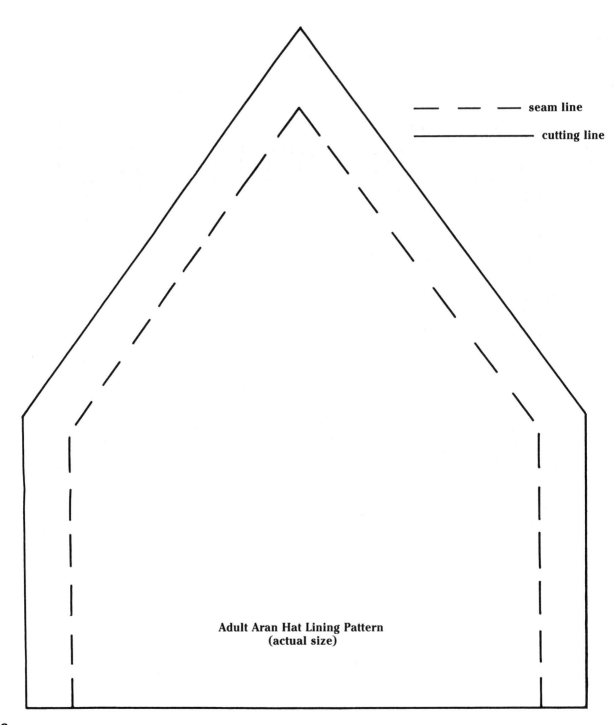

— — — seam line

———————— cutting line

Adult Aran Hat Lining Pattern
(actual size)

His and Hers Diamond-patterned Pullovers and Coordinated Accessories

These adaptations of traditional argyle patterns have a sparkling fresh look that is obviously becoming to both sexes. It is their difference in pattern and scale, combined with their color coordination that makes the sweaters so subtly pleasing. The scarf and cap are interchangeable for either sex.

Lady's Diamond Turtleneck

SIZES: Directions for small size (6–8). Changes for medium size (10–12) and large size (14–16) are in parentheses.

Body Bust Size: 30½"–31½" (32½"–34"; 36"–38")

MATERIALS: Bulky yarn, 6 (6–7) 1⁶⁄₁₀-oz. balls natural, main color (MC); 2 (3–3) balls light beige (A), 2 (2–3) balls each of medium brown (B) and dark brown (C). Knitting needles, Nos. 8 and 10. Two stitch holders.

GAUGE: 7 sts = 2", 28 rows (1 pat) = 6" (No. 10 needles).

PATTERN NOTES: Always change colors on wrong side, picking up new strand from under dropped strand. Carry colors not being used loosely across back of work; when more than 3 sts between colors, twist strands after every 3rd st. Cut and join colors when necessary.

PULLOVER BACK: Beg at lower edge, with MC and No. 8 needles, cast on 55 (61–67) sts.

Ribbing

Row 1 (right side): K 1, * p 1, k 1, repeat from * across.

Row 2: P 1, * k 1, p 1, repeat from * across. Repeat these 2 rows for 3″, end wrong side, inc 6 sts evenly spaced on last row—61 (67–73) sts. Change to No. 10 needles.

PATTERN

Row 1 (right side): Following Chart 1, k from A to B once, from B to C 10 (11–12) times.

Row 2: P from C to B 10 (11–12) times, from B to A once. Repeat these 2 rows to top of chart (18 rows).

Rows 19–28: With MC, work in stockinette st (k 1 row, p 1 row). Repeat these 28 rows for pat until piece measures 16″ (16½″–17″) from start or desired length to underarm. Mark each side of last row for underarm. Piece above ribbing should measure 17½″ (19″–20¾″) wide. Keeping to pat as established, work even until armholes measure 7″ (7¾″–8¼″) above underarm markers.

Shape Shoulders: Bind off 20 (22–24) sts, work in pat as established on next 21 (23–25) sts; sl these sts on a holder, bind off remaining 20 (22–24) sts.

FRONT: Work same as for back until armholes measure 5″ (5½″–6″) above underarm markers.

Shape Neck: Keeping to pat as established, work 26 (28–30) sts, drop yarn, sl center 9 (11–13) sts on a holder; join another strand of color to be used, finish row. Working on both sides at once, with separate strands of yarn, dec 1 st at each neck edge every row 3 times, then every other row 3 times—20 (22–24) sts

☐ MC
☒ A
◉ B
☑ C

Chart 1   Chart 2

each side. Work even until armholes measure same as back. Bind off.

Sew left shoulder seam.

Turtleneck: From right side, with MC and No. 8 needles, k across sts on back holder, pick up and k 15 sts across left front neck edge, k across sts on front holder, pick up and k 16 sts on right front neck edge—61 (65–69) sts. Work in ribbing same as for back for 6″. Bind off loosely in ribbing.

Sew right shoulder and turtleneck seam.

SLEEVES: From right side, with B and No. 10 needles, pick up and k 49 (55–61) sts across armhole edge of back and front, from marker to marker. P 1 row.

PATTERN

Row 1 (right side): Following Chart 2, beg with row 3, k from A to B once, from B to C 8 (9–10) times.

Row 2: P from C to B 8 (9–10) times, from B to A once. Repeat last 2 rows to top of chart, then working with MC only, work in stockinette st for 10 rows; **at the same time,** dec 1 st each side every 2″ once. Repeating the 18 rows of chart and 10 MC rows, work in pat until 18 rows of 3rd pat are completed; **at the same time,** continue to dec 1 st each side every 2″ (1¾″–1½″) 4 (5–6) times—39 (43–47) sts. Change to No. 8 needles. With MC, k 1 row, dec 10 sts evenly spaced across—29 (33–37) sts. Work in ribbing same as for back for 3″. Bind off loosely in ribbing. Work other sleeve in same manner.

FINISHING: Block pullover. Sew side and sleeve seams.

Scarf and Cap

SIZE: Scarf: 7½" × 56", plus fringe. Cap: One size fits all.

MATERIALS: Bulky yarn. For Set: 6 1⁶⁄₁₀-oz. balls natural, main color (MC); 1 ball each of light brown (A), medium brown (B), and dark brown (C). For Solid Color Scarf only: 5 balls MC. Knitting needles, No. 10.

GAUGE: 7 sts = 2" (stockinette st.)

PATTERN NOTES: Same as for Lady's Turtleneck.

Cap

Cuff: With MC, cast on 67 sts. Work in ribbing of k 1, p 1 for 3 rows.

PATTERN

Row 1: Following Chart 2, k from A to B once, from B to C across.

Row 2: P from C to B across, end p from B to A once. Repeat last 2 rows to top of chart (18 rows). Working with MC only, k 1 row.

Crown

Row 1: K 1, * p 1, k 1, repeat from * across.

Row 2: P 1, * k 1, p 1, repeat from * across. Work in ribbing as established until crown measures 9" above cuff, end row 1.

Shape Top

Next Row: * Sl 1, k 1, psso, repeat from * across, end k 1—34 sts. P 1 row.

Next Row: * Sl 1, k 1, psso, repeat from * across. Cut yarn, leaving a long end for sewing. Draw yarn through remaining 17 sts. Fasten securely on wrong side; weave back seam. Fold first 3 rows of ribbing to wrong side of cuff; hem in place. Turn cuff to right side. With MC, make pompom; sew to top of cap.

Scarf

Note: For solid color fringe, cut 92 12" MC strands. For colored fringe, cut 16 12" MC strands.

With MC, cast on 45 sts.

Row 1 (wrong side): P 1, * k 1, p 1, repeat from * across.

Row 2: K 1, * p 1, k 1, repeat from * across. Repeat these 2 rows until all MC yarn is used. Bind off in ribbing same tension as sts.

FRINGE: Using tapestry needle and from right side, knot 2 strands MC in every k st across each end of scarf. For multi-colored fringe, knot yarn in following color sequence: B, A, MC, A, B, *C, B, A, MC, A, B, repeat from * twice.

Man's Diamond-patterned Sweater

SIZES: Directions for size 38. Changes for sizes 40, 42, and 44 are in parentheses.

Body Chest Size: 38" (40"–42"–44")

Blocked Chest Size: 39½" (42"–44"–46")

MATERIALS: Bulky yarn, 9 (10–11–12) 1⁶⁄₁₀-oz. balls natural, main color (MC); 1 ball each of dark brown (A), medium brown (B), and beige (C). Knitting needles, Nos. 8 and 10. Thirteen bobbins. Two stitch holders.

GAUGE: 7 sts = 2"; 5 rows = 1" (No. 10 needles)

PATTERN NOTES: Use a separate bobbin for each diamond color change and each MC section. When starting new diamonds, carry yarn of previous diamond in back of work until previous diamond is completed. Always change colors on wrong side, picking up new strand from under dropped strand. Wind 4 MC bobbins, 3 bobbins each of A, B and C. Cut and join colors as needed.

SWEATER BACK: Beg at lower edge, with MC and No. 8 needles, cast on 65 (69–73–77) sts.

Ribbing

Row 1 (right side): K 1, * p 1, k 1, repeat from * across.

Row 2: P 1, * k 1, p 1, repeat from * across. Repeat these 2 rows for 3" (3"–3½"–3½"), end wrong side, inc 4 sts evenly spaced across last row—69 (73–77–81) sts. Change to No. 10

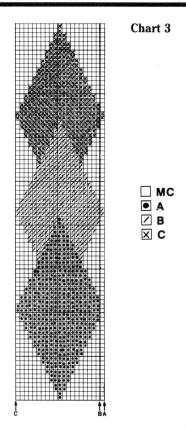

Chart 3

☐ MC
◉ A
☑ B
☒ C

needles. Work in stockinette st (k 1 row, p 1 row) for 74 rows, end p row. Piece above ribbing should measure 19¾" (21"–22"–23") wide.

Shape Armholes: Bind off 4 sts at beg of next 2 rows. Dec 1 st each side every other row 3 times—55 (59–63–67) sts. Work even until armholes measure 8¼" (8¾"–9¼"–9½") above first bound-off sts.

Shape Shoulders: Bind off 5 (5–6–6) sts at beg of next 4 (2–6–4) rows, 6 (6–0–7) sts next 2 (4–0–2) rows. Sl remaining 23 (25–27–29) sts on a holder.

FRONT: Cast on and work ribbing same as for back, inc 4 sts evenly spaced across last row—69 (73–77–81) sts. Change to No. 10 needles.

PATTERN

Row 1 (right side): K 4 (6–8–10) MC; following Chart 3, k from A to B once, from B to C 3 times; k 4 (6–8–10) MC.

Row 2: P 4 (6–8–10) MC; following chart, p from C to B 3 times, from B to A once; p 4 (6–8–10). Repeat last 2 rows to end of row 74.

Shape Armholes: Keeping to pat as established, bind off 4 sts at beg of next 2 rows. Dec 1 st each side every other row 3 times—55 (59–63–67) sts. Work to top of chart, then working with MC only, work even until armholes measure 5¼" (5¾"–6¼"–6½") above first bound-off sts, end p row.

Shape Neck: K 22 (23–24–25), drop yarn, sl center 11 (13–15–17) sts on a holder; join another strand of MC, k 22 (23–24–25). Working on both sides at once, with separate strands of yarn, dec 1 st at each neck edge every row 3 times, then every other row 3 times—16 (17–18–19) sts each side. Work even until armholes measure same as back.

Shape Shoulders: Bind off 5 (6–6–6) sts at beg of each arm side 2 (2–3–2) times, 6 (5–0–7) sts once.

SLEEVES: Beg at lower edge, with MC and No. 8 needles, cast on 33 (35–37–39) sts. Work in ribbing same as for back for 3" (3"–3½"–3½"), end wrong side, inc 8 sts evenly spaced across last row—41 (43–45–47) sts. Change to No. 10 needles. Work in stockinette st, inc 1 st each side every 10th row 6 times—53 (55–57–59) sts. Work even until piece measures 19" (19"–19½"–19½") from start or desired length to underarm, end p row. Piece above last inc row should measure 15" (15½"–16"–16½") wide.

Shape Cap: Bind off 4 sts at beg of next 2 rows. Dec 1 st each side every other row 14 (15–16–17) times. Bind off 2 sts at beg of next 4 rows. Bind off remaining 9 sts.

FINISHING: Run in yarn ends on wrong side. Block pieces. Sew left shoulder seam.

Neckband: From right side, with MC and No. 8 needles, k across sts on back st holder, pick up and k 16 sts on left front neck edge, k across sts on front holder, pick up and k 17 sts on right front neck edge—67 (71–75–79) sts. Beg with row 2, work in ribbing same as for back for 2½". Bind off loosely in ribbing.

Sew right shoulder and neckband seam. Fold neckband in half to wrong side; hem in place. Sew in sleeves. Sew side and sleeve seams.

A Cabled, Shawl-collared Sweater For the Man in Your Life

Nothing becomes a man more than a handsome hand-knit sweater, and this richly cabled cardigan is particularly attractive because it looks and feels wonderful both indoors and out.

SIZES: Directions are for size 38. Changes for sizes 40, 42 and 44 are in parentheses.

Body Chest Size: 38″ (40″–42″–44″)

Blocked Chest Size: 39″ (41″–43″–45″)

MATERIALS: Bulky yarn, 15 (16–17–18) 1.6-oz. balls. Knitting needles, Nos. 8 and 10 (5 and 6 mm). One dp needle. Six buttons. Stitch holder.

GAUGE: 7 sts = 2″; 5 rows = 1″, rib pat on No. 10 needles. 16 sts = 3″, cable pat on No. 10 needles.

CABLE PATTERN: Worked on 18 sts

Row 1 (right side): P 1, k 16, p 1.

Row 2 and All Even Rows: K the k sts, p the p sts.

Row 3: P 1, sl next 4 sts to dp needle, hold in back of work, k 4, k 4 from dp needle (RC); sl next 4 sts to dp needle, hold in front of work, k 4, k 4 from dp needle, p 1.

Rows 5 and 7: Repeat row 1.

Row 9: P 1, sl next 4 sts to dp needle, hold in front of work, k 2, p 2, k 4 from dp needle; sl next 4 sts to dp needle, hold in back of work, k 4, p 2, k 2 from dp needle, p 1.

Row 11: P 1, k 2, p 2, k 8, p 2, k 2, p 1.

Row 13: P 1, k 2, p 2, RC, p 2, k 2, p 1.

Row 15: Repeat row 11.

Row 17: Repeat row 13.

Row 19: Repeat row 11. Repeat rows 3–20 for pat st.

CARDIGAN BACK: Beg at lower edge, with No. 8 needles, cast on 67 (71–75–79) sts.

Row 1 (right side): K 1, * p 1, k 1, repeat from * across.

Row 2: P 1, * k 1, p 1, repeat from * across. Repeat these 2 rows for ribbing for 3″, inc 12 sts evenly spaced across last row—79 (83–87–91) sts. Change to No. 10 needles.

PATTERN

Row 1 (right side): P 0 (0–2–2), (k 2, p 2) 2 times, k 2, row 1 of cable pat over 18 sts, p 1, k 2, (p 2, k 2) 5 (6–6–7) times, row 1 of cable pat over 18 sts, p 1, (k 2, p 2) 2 times, k 1 (1–2–2), p 0 (0–1–1).

Row 2: K 0 (0–2–2), p 2, (k 2, p 2) 2 times, row 2 of cable pat over 18 sts, k 1, p 2 (k 2, p 2) 5 (6–6–7) times, row 2 of cable pat over 18 sts, k 1, (p 2, k 2) 2 times, p 1 (1–2–2), k 0 (0–1–1).

Row 3: P 0 (0–2–2), (k 2, p 2) 2 times, k 2, row 3 of cable pat over 18 sts, p 1, k 2, (p 2, k 2) 5 (6–6–7) times, row 3 of cable pat over 18 sts, k 1, (p 2, k 2) 2 times, p 1 (1–2–2), k 0 (0–1–1).

Row 4: K 0 (0–2–2), p 2, (k 2, p 2) 2 times, row 4 of cable pat over 18 sts, k 1, p 2, (k 2, p 2) 5 (6–6–7) times, row 4 of cable pat over 18 sts, k 1, (p 2, k 2) 2 times, p 1 (1–2–2), k 0 (0–1–1). Continue in established pats, keeping broken rib pat at sides and center and 18 cable panel sts as established. Work until 17″ from start or desired length to underarm. Check gauge; piece should measure 19½″ (21½″–22½″–23½″) wide.

Shape Armholes: Keeping to pat, bind off 2 sts at beg of next 2 rows. Dec 1 st each side every other row 2 times—71 (75–79–83) sts. Work until armholes measure 8¾″ (9¼″–9¾″–10¼″) above bound-off sts.

Shape Shoulders: Keeping to pat, bind off 8 (8–9–9) sts at beg of next 4 rows, 7 (8–8–9) sts at beg of next 2 rows. Bind off remaining 25 (27–27–29) sts for back of neck.

POCKET LININGS (make 2): With No. 10 needles, cast on 28 sts. Work in stockinette st (k 1 row, p 1 row) for 6″. Sl sts on a holder.

RIGHT FRONT: Beg at lower edge, with No. 8 needles, cast on 41 (43–45–47) sts. Work rib border same as back for 3″, inc 6 sts evenly spaced across first 30 (32–34–36) sts on last row—47 (49–51–53) sts. Change to No. 10 needles.

PATTERN

Row 1 (right side): Rib 9 as established (front band), k 2 (0–0–2), (p 2, k 2) 2 (3–3–3) times, row 1 of cable pat over 18 sts, k 1, (p 2, k 2) 2 times, p 1 (1–2–2), k 0 (0–1–1).

Row 2: Broken rib pat over first 10 (10–12–12) sts, row 2 of cable pat over 18 sts, broken rib to last 9 sts, rib 9. Keeping pats as established, work until 2nd row 10 of cable pat has been completed.

Pocket Opening

Next Row: Keeping to pat, work 14 (16–16–18) sts, work next 28 sts and sl on a holder for pocket border, finish row.

Next Row: Work to sts on holder; holding k side of pocket lining to wrong side of work, p across 28 sts from one pocket lining holder, finish row. Continue until piece measures same as back to underarm, ending at front edge.

Shape Neck and Armhole

Row 1 (right side): Rib 9 sts, inc 1 st in next st, finish row.

Row 2: Bind off 2 sts, work in pat to last 11 sts, rib to end.

Row 3: Rib 11, inc 1 st in next st, work in pat to last 2 sts, dec 1 st. Dec 1 st at armhole edge every other row once more; **at the same time,** inc 1 st inside collar edge, working 2 sts more in rib pat, every other row 6 (7–7–8) times—25 (27–27–29) sts in collar rib; 26 (27–29–30) pat sts.

Next Row: Rib 25 (27–27–29) sts from collar edge, inc 1 st in next st, finish row. Continue to inc 1 st inside collar edge every other row 10 (6–6–3) times, every 4th row 0 (2–2–3) times, always working new sts in rib pat—36 collar rib sts. Work until piece measures same as back to shoulder.

Shape Shoulder: Bind off 9 (9–10–10) sts at armhole edge twice, 8 (9–9–10) sts once. Rib on remaining 36 sts for collar until piece measures to center back of neck. Bind off in ribbing.

With pins, mark position of 6 buttons evenly spaced on right front border: first one 1″ from lower edge, last one 1″ below start of collar.

LEFT FRONT: Work to correspond to right front, reversing shaping and pat, working buttonholes opposite markers.

Buttonhole Row: Work to 6 sts from front edge, bind off 3 sts, finish row.

Next Row: Work in pat, casting on 3 sts over bound-off sts.

SLEEVES: Beg at lower edge, with No. 8 needles, cast on 33 (35–37–39) sts. Work in ribbing of k 1, p 1 for 3″, inc 10 sts evenly spaced across last row—43 (45–47–49) sts. Change to No. 10 needles.

PATTERN

Row 1 (right side): * K 2, p 2, repeat from * to last 3 (1–3–1) sts, k 2 (1–2–1), p 1 (0–1–0).

Row 2: K 2 (0–2–0), * p 2, k 2, repeat from * across, end p 1. Repeat these 2 rows for pat. Work 10 rows. Inc 1 st each side of next row, then every 10th row 6 times working added sts into pat—57 (59–61–63) sts. Work until piece measures 19″ (19″–20″–20″) from start or desired length to underarm. Piece should measure 16″ (16¾″–17½″–18″) wide.

Shape Cap: Keeping to pat, bind off 4 sts at beg of next 2 rows. Dec 1 st each side every other row 14 (15–16–17) times. Bind off 2 sts at beg of next 2 rows. Bind off remaining 17 sts.

FINISHING: Sew side and sleeve seams. Sew in sleeves. Weave collar at center back of neck. Sew collar to back of neck, having center back of collar about 1″ below neck edge and tapering to shoulder seams.

Pocket Border: From right side, pick up and k 28 sts from pocket holder onto No. 8 needles, inc 1 st—29 sts. Work in ribbing of k 1, p 1 for 6 rows. Bind off loosely in ribbing. Tack edges of pocket border to front. Sew pocket linings in place. Sew on buttons.

Infant's Ice Cream Cone Suit, Hat, Booties, Toy, and Blanket

Here is a suit and accessory set for baby that looks good enough to eat. The triple-dip cone on the blanket is appliquéd.

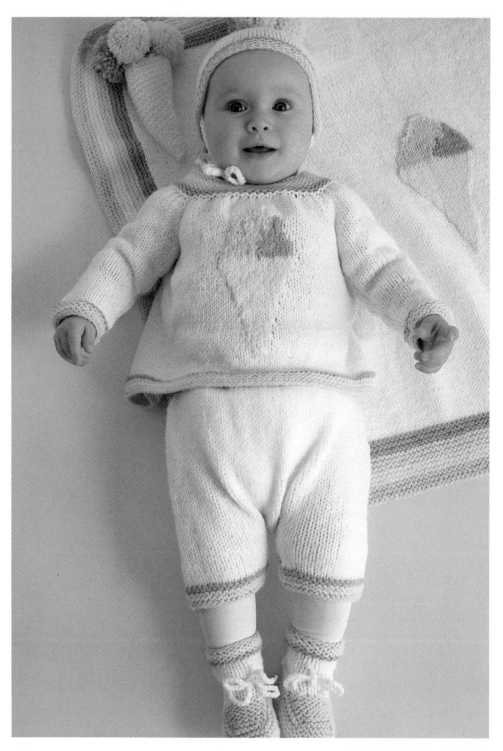

SIZE: Directions for size 6 months. Changes for size 1 year are in parentheses. Coverlet, 25″ × 30″.

Body Chest Size: Up to 19″ (20″)

Blocked Chest Size: 22½″ (24½″)

MATERIALS: Sport Yarn, 2-oz. skeins, 5 skeins white (A) and 1 skein each mint (B), pale yellow (C), pale pink (D), and blue (E). Knitting needles, Nos. 5 and 6 (3¾ and 4¼ mm). 5 stitch holders. Small Velcro® fastener for sweater. Elastic thread for pants. Crochet hook for hat and bootie ties.

GAUGE: 21 sts = 4″; 40 rows (20 ridges) = 4″ (garter st, No. 5 needles). 20 sts = 4″; 27 rows = 4″ (stockinette st, No. 6 needles).

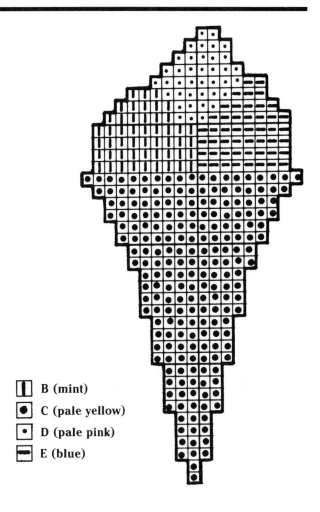

B (mint)
C (pale yellow)
D (pale pink)
E (blue)

Ice Cream Cone Suit

SWEATER BODY: Beg at lower edge, with B and No. 5 needles, cast on 114 (122) sts. Work in garter st (k each row) working 2 rows (1 ridge) each of B, C, D and E. Change to No. 6 needles. Work in stockinette st (k 1 row, p 1 row) with A for 8 (10) rows.

PATTERN

Row 1 (right side): With A, k 57 (61) sts; join C and k 1; with A finish row. Continue to follow chart for ice cream cone motif until piece measures 7½″ (8″) from start, ending with a p row.

Divide Work

Next Row (right side): With A, k 32 (34) sts; join another ball of A and bind off next 4 sts for underarm; continue to follow chart until 42 (46) sts beyond bound-off sts; join another ball of A and bind off next 4 sts for underarm, finish row. Working each section separately with a separate ball of yarn, dec 1 st at each armhole edge of backs and front every other row 3 (4) times, continuing to work front to top of chart, then working with A only. After last dec, sl remaining 29 (30) sts on each half of back on separate holders and remaining 36 (38) sts of front on another holder.

SLEEVES: With B and No. 5 needles, cast on 30 (32) sts. Work in garter st, working 2 rows (1 ridge) each of B, C, D and E. Change to No. 6 needles. Work in stockinette st with A, inc 1 st each side every 10 (8) rows 4 (5) times—38 (42) sts. Work even until sleeve measures 7½″ (8″) from start.

Shape Cap: Bind off 2 sts at beg of next 2 rows. Dec 1 st each edge every other row 3 (4) times, end p row. Sl remaining 28 (30) sts onto a holder.

Yoke: From right side, sl 29 (30) sts of left half of back, 28 (30) sts of one sleeve, 36 (38) sts of front, 28 (30) sts of other sleeve and 29 (30) sts of right half of back onto No. 5 needles—150 (158) sts.

Row 1 (right side): With A, k 2 tog across row—75 (79) sts.

Row 2: With A, k. Continue in garter st, working 4 rows (2 ridges) each E, D, C and B, binding off all sts on last row.

FINISHING: Sew sleeve seams and armhole seams. Place a piece of Velcro® fastener on each half of back at upper center edge.

Pants

BACK

First Leg: Beg at lower edge, with B and No. 5 needles, cast on 21 (23) sts. Work in garter st, working 2 rows (1 ridge) each of B, C, D and E. Change to No. 6 needles. Work in stockinette st with A for 4 rows. Continue in stockinette st with A, inc 1 st at end of every k row 3 times, then cast on 5 sts at same edge for crotch. Leave the 29 (31) sts on a holder.

Second Leg: Work to correspond to first leg, working incs at end of p rows.

Upper Portion

Next Row (right side): With 1 ball of A and No. 6 needles, k across sts of first leg and 2nd leg—58 (62) sts. Work in stockinette st for 6″ (6½″).

Waistband

Next Row (right side): With A, k 2 tog, (k 5, k 2 tog) 8 times, end k 0 (4)—49 (53) sts.

Next Row: With A, p. Change to No. 5 needles. Work in garter st, working 2 rows (1 ridge) each E, D, C and B. Bind off.

FRONT: Work same as back.

FINISHING: Sew side and leg seams. Run 2 rows of elastic thread through back side of waistband stitches, bringing waist in to desired fit.

HAT: With B and No. 5 needles, cast on 60 (64) sts. Work in garter st, working 2 rows (1 ridge) each B, C, D and E. Change to No. 6 needles. Work in stockinette st with A until 3″ (3¼″) from start, end p row.

Next Row (right side): (K 8, k 2 tog) 6 times, end k 0 (4)—54 (58) sts. P 1 row, k 1 row, p 1 row.

Next Row: (K 8, k 2 tog) 5 times, end k 4 (8)—49 (53) sts.

Next Row: Purl.

Next Row: (K 6, k 2 tog) 6 times, end k 1 (5)—43 (47) sts.

Next Row: Purl.

Next Row: (K 6, k 2 tog) 5 times, end k 3 (7)—38 (42) sts.

Next Row: Purl.

Next Row: (K 5, k 2 tog) 5 (6) times, end k 3 (0)—33 (36) sts.

Next Row: Purl.

Next Row: (K 5, k 2 tog) 4 (5) times, end k 5 (1)—29 (31) sts.

Next Row: Purl. Continue with A in stockinette st until 4¾″ (5″) from start.

PATTERN

With E and No. 5 needles, k 2 rows.

Next Row: With E, (k 3, k 2 tog) 5 (6) times, end k 4 (1)—24 (25) sts.

Next Row: With E, k. With D, k 2 rows.

Next Row: With D, (k 3, k 2 tog) 4 (5) times, end k 4 (0)—20 sts.

Next Row: With D, k. With C, k 2 rows.

Next Row: With C, (k 2, tog) 5 times—15 sts.

Next Row: With C, k. With B, k 2 rows.

Next Row: With B, (k 2, k 2 tog) 3 times, end k 3—12 sts.

Next Row: With B, k.

Next Row: With B, k 2 sts tog across row—6 sts. Cut yarn, leaving an 8″ end. Draw end through remaining 6 sts and end off.

FINISHING: Sew hat seam.

Pompoms: Make 1 pompom each of B, D and E 2″ in diameter. Sew to top of hat.

Ties: With A, crochet 2 chains each 13″ long. Sew a tie to each side of hat.

Booties (make 2)

With No. 5 needles and B, cast on 25 (29) sts. Work in garter st, working 2 rows (1 ridge) each B, C, D and E. Change to A and No. 6 needles. Work in stockinette st for 1¼″ (1½″), end p row.

Eyelet Row (right side): (K 2 tog, yo) across row, end k 1.

Next Row: P all sts and yo's—25 (29) sts. Continue in stockinette st with A until 2¼″ (2½″) in A section, end p row.

Shape Instep

Next Row (right side): Sl first 9 (10) sts onto holder, join B and k center 7 (9) sts, sl last 9 (10) sts onto another holder. Continue on center 7 (9) sts in garter st with B until 14 (16) rows are completed.

FOOT

Next Row (right side): With B, k 9 (10) sts from first holder, pick up and k 8 (9) sts on side of instep, k across 7 (9) sts of instep, pick up and k 8 (9) sts on other side of instep, k 9 (10) sts from 2nd holder—41 (47) sts. Working in garter st, work 4 rows (2 ridges) each B, C and D.

Shape Sole: Change to E and stockinette st.

Row 1 (right side): K 3 (4), k 2 tog, k 11 (12), k 2 tog, k 5 (7), k 2 tog, k 11 (12), k 2 tog, k 3 (4)—37 (43) sts.

Rows 2 and 4: Purl.

Row 3: K 3 (4), k 2 tog, k 9 (10), k 2 tog, k 5 (7), k 2 tog, k 9 (10), k 2 tog, k 3 (4)—33 (39) sts.

Row 5: K 2 (3), k 2 tog, k 9 (10), k 2 tog, k 3 (5), k 2 tog, k 9 (10), k 2 tog, k 2 (3)—29 (35) sts.

Row 6: Purl.

Row 7: P and bind off remaining 29 (35) sts. Work 2nd bootie the same way.

FINISHING: Sew back and sole seam.

Ties (make 2): With A, ch 80. End off. Insert ties through eyelet row of booties.

Coverlet

With No. 5 needles and B, cast on 130 sts. Working in garter st, working 6 rows (3 ridges) each of B, C, D and E, dec 1 st each side every 4th row 3 times—124 sts. Change to No. 6 needles. Work in stockinette st with A until coverlet measures 24″ from start. Change to No. 5 needles. Working in garter st, working 6 rows (3 ridges) each of E, D, C and B, inc 1 st each side every 4th row 3 times—130 sts. Bind off loosely.

Side Edging: Along one A side of coverlet, with No. 5 needles and E, pick up and k 124 sts. Work in garter st, working 6 rows (3 ridges) each E, D, C and B, inc 1 st each side every 4th row 3 times—130 sts. Bind off. Work same edging along other A side of coverlet. Join corners.

Ice Cream Cone Motif: Following chart, knit a separate ice cream cone motif and sew to center of coverlet with invisible stitches as illustrated.

Toy

With No. 5 needles and C, cast on 4 sts. Working in garter st, work even for 4 rows, then inc 1 st each side every other row 3 times, then every 4 rows 8 times—26 sts. Work even until piece is 4″ long. Bind off 3 sts at beg of next 6 rows. Bind off remaining 8 sts.

FINISHING: Fold piece in half vertically and sew into a cone. Stuff cone.

Pompoms: Make 1 pompom each of B, D and E 2″ in diameter. Stitch in place on top of cone.

Sweetheart Cardigan and Pullover For the Young Set

Capture the heart of your young valentine with a sweetheart cardigan or pullover. The cardigan has stylishly puffed sleeves for a feminine touch, while the one-piece pullover is suitable for either sex.

SIZES: Directions are for size 4. Changes for sizes 6 and 8 are in parentheses.

Body Chest Size: 23″ (25″–27″)

Blocked Chest Size: 26″ (28″–30″)

MATERIALS: Knitting Worsted, 6 (8–10) ozs. red (A), 4 (4–6) ozs. white (B). Knitting needles, Nos. 4 and 6 (3½ and 4¼ mm). 5 stitch holders. Six buttons.

GAUGE: 5 sts = 1″; 7 rows = 1″

Pattern Notes: Always change colors on wrong side, picking up new strand from under dropped strand. Carry unused color across loosely, twisting every 4th stitch between colors. Cut and join colors as needed.

Sweetheart Cardigan

CARDIGAN BACK Beg at lower edge, with No. 4 needles and A, cast on 62 (66–72) sts. Work in ribbing of k 1, p 1 for 1¾″. Change to No. 6 needles and stockinette st (k 1 row, p 1 row). Work 2 rows A, inc 1 st on first row—63 (67–73) sts.

PATTERN

Following chart for back work from A to B through row 14, then repeat rows 5–14 until piece measures 8″ (8½″–9½″) from start, or 1″ less than desired length to underarm. Piece should measure 12½″ (13½″–14½″) wide. Work 6 rows of pat as shown on chart.

Shape Armholes: Keeping to pat, bind off 2 sts at beg of next 2 rows. Dec 1 st each edge every other row twice—55 (59–65) sts. Work until armholes measure 4¾″ (5¼″–5¾″) above bound-off sts.

Shape Shoulders: Bind off 9 (10–10) sts at beg of next 2 rows, 9 (9–11) sts at beg of next 2 rows. Sl remaining 19 (21–23) sts on holder.

LEFT FRONT: Beg at lower edge, with No. 4 needles and A, cast on 32 (34–36) sts. Work in ribbing of k 1, p 1 for 1¾″. Change to No. 6 needles and stockinette st. Work 2 rows A, inc 0 (0–1) st on first row—32 (34–37) sts.

PATTERN

Row 1 (right side): Following chart, k from A to C.

Row 2: P from C to A. Repeat last 2 rows until piece has same number of pat rows as back to underarm, end at side edge. Piece should measure 6½″ (7″–7½″) wide.

Shape Armhole: Keeping to pat, bind off 2 sts at side edge once. Dec 1 st at same edge every other row twice—28 (30–33) sts. Work until armhole measures 3¼″ (4″–4½″) above bound-off sts, ending at front edge.

Shape Neck

Next Row: Work first 10 sts and sl on a holder, finish row. Continue in pat, dec 1 st at neck edge every row 0 (1–2) times—18 (19–21) sts. Work until armhole measures 4¾″ (5¼″–5¾″) above first bound-off sts.

Shape Shoulder: Bind off 9 (10–10) sts at beg of side edge once, 9 (9–11) sts once.

RIGHT FRONT: Work as for left front to beg of pat.

PATTERN

Row 1 (right side): Following chart, k from D to B.

Row 2: P from B to D. Complete to correspond to left front, reversing shaping.

SLEEVES: Beg at lower edge, with No. 4 needles and A, cast on 36 (40–46) sts. Work in ribbing of k 1, p 1 for 2¼″ (2½″–2¾″). Change to No. 6 needles and stockinette st. Work 2 rows A, inc 5 sts evenly spaced across first row—41 (45–51) sts.

PATTERN

Row 1 (right side): Following chart for sleeves, k from A to B.

Row 2: P from B to A. Repeat last 2 rows, inc 1 st each side every 6th row 4 times working added sts into pat—49 (53–59) sts. Work until sleeve measures 9½″ (10½″–11½″) or 1″ less than desired length to underarm, repeating snowflake pat as necessary, then work last 6 rows of pat to underarm. Piece should measure 9¾″ (10½″–11¾″) wide.

Shape Cap: Keeping to pat, bind off 3 sts at beg of next 2 rows. Dec 1 st each side every other row twice—39 (43–49) sts. Work until

Cardigan Back and fronts

□ A
◉ B

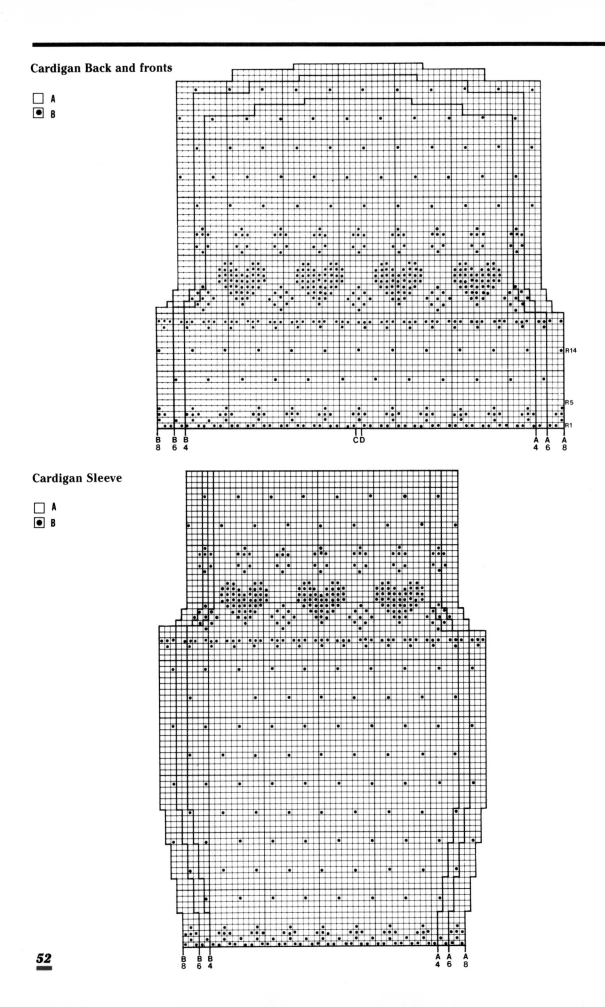

R14

R5
R1

B B B
8 6 4

C D

A A A
4 6 8

Cardigan Sleeve

□ A
◉ B

B B B
8 6 4

A A A
4 6 8

cap measures 4¾" (5¼"–5¾") above first bound-off sts.

Next Row (right side): * With A, sl 2, k 3 tog, pass 2 sl sts over, repeat from *, end sl 2 (1–2), k 2 tog, pass 2 (1–2) sl sts over. Bind off remaining sts.

FINISHING: Sew shoulder, side and sleeve seams, matching pats. Sew in sleeves easing in fullness at top.

Button Band: With No. 4 needles and A, cast on 8 sts. Work in ribbing of k 1, p 1 until band reaches from bottom edge to neck edge. Sl sts on a holder. With pins, mark position of 5 buttons evenly spaced on band, first one 1" above lower edge; 6th button will be in neckband.

Buttonhole Band: Work as for button band for 1".

Buttonhole Row: Work 3, bind off 2 sts, finish row.

Next Row: Work in ribbing casting on 2 sts over bound-off sts. Continue in ribbing working button-holes opposite markers. When band measures same as button band, sl sts onto a holder.

Sew button band to left front and buttonhole band to right front for girl; button band to right front and buttonhole band to left front for boy.

Neckband: From right side, with No. 4 needles and A, pick up and k 76 (78–80) sts around neck edge including sts on holders. Work in ribbing of k 1, p 1 for 2 rows. Work 6th buttonhole in buttonhole band. Work in ribbing for 3 more rows. Bind off loosely in ribbing. Sew on buttons.

Sweetheart Pullover

SIZES: Directions are for size 4. Changes for sizes 6 and 8 are in parentheses.

Body Chest Size: 23" (25"–27")

Blocked Chest Size: 26" (27½"–29")

MATERIALS: Knitting Worsted 8 (10–12) ozs. red (A), 4 (6–6) ozs, white (B). Circular needles, Nos. 4 and 6 (3½ and 4¼ mm). Set dp needles, Nos. 4 and 6 (3½ and 4¼ mm).

GAUGE: 5 sts = 1"; 7 rows = 1".

Pattern Notes: Always change colors on wrong side, picking up new strand from under dropped strand. Carry unused color across loosely; when more than 3 sts between colors, twist every 3rd st. Cut and join colors when necessary.

PULLOVER BODY: Beg at neck edge, with No. 4 dp needles and A, cast on 78 (80–82) sts. Divide sts on 3 dp needles. Join, being careful not to twist sts. Mark beg of rnd. Work around in ribbing of k 1, p 1 for 1". Change to No. 6 dp needles.

Next rnd: K, inc 34 (36–38) sts evenly spaced around—112 (116–120) sts.

Yoke: Following Chart 1, work in stockinette st (k each rnd), repeating from A to B around for 3 rnds. Change to No. 6 circular needle.

Inc rnd: * With B, k 4 (4–5), inc 1 st in next st, repeat from * 19 times, end k 12 (16–0)—132 (136–140) sts. Work next 3 rnds of pat on Chart 1.

Inc rnd: * With B, k 5 (5–6), inc 1 st in next st, repeat from * 19 times, end k 12 (16–0)—152 (156–160) sts. Work next 3 rnds of pat on Chart 1.

Inc rnd: * With B, k 8 (5–7), inc 1 st in next st, repeat from * 15 (23–19) times, end k 8 (12–0)—168 (180–180) sts. Work 0 (0–1) rnd with B. Follow Chart 2 for next 12 rnds, repeat from A to B around.

Inc rnd: *With B, k 7 (10–8), inc 1 st in next st, repeat from * 19 (15–19) times, end k 8 (4–0)—188 (196–200) sts. With B, k 0 (0–1) rnd. Follow Chart 3 for next 3 rnds of pat, repeat from A to B around.

Inc rnd: * With B, k 10 (8–7), inc 1 st in next st, repeat from * 15 (19–23) times, end k 12 (16–8)—204 (216–224) sts.

For sizes 6 and 8 only: Work next 3 rnds of pat on Chart 3.
With B, k 0 (0–1) rnd.

Inc rnd: * With B, k 9 (8–6), inc 1 st in next

st, repeat from * 19 (23–31) times, end k 4 (0–0)—224 (240–256) sts. With B, k 0 (0–1) rnd.

For all sizes: Work 5 rnds of Chart 4, repeating from A to B around.

Divide Yoke

Next rnd: With A and No. 6 circular needle, k 63 (67–71) sts for back, inc 1 st at center, place next 49 (53–57) sts on a holder for sleeve, cast on 1 (1–0) st, k next 63 (67–71) sts for front, inc 1 st at center, place next 49 (53–57) sts on a holder for sleeve, cast on 1 (1–0) st—130 (138–144) sts. Piece should measure 26″ (27½″–29″) around. Join and work around in stockinette st for 3 rnds.

For size 4 only: Follow Chart 5, repeat from A to B around.

For size 6 only: Follow Chart 6, repeat from A to B around 11 times, ending at C.

For size 8 only: Follow Chart 6, repeat from A to B around.
Continue as established until piece

measures 6¾″ (7¾″–9¼″) from underarm or desired length to top of waist ribbing.

Next rnd: With A, k , dec 8 (10–10) sts evenly spaced around—122 (128–134) sts. Change to No. 4 circular needle. Work in ribbing of k 1, p 1 for 1¾″. Bind off in ribbing.

SLEEVES: Divide 49 (53–57) sleeve sts on 3 No. 6 dp needles, cast on 1 (1–3) sts at underarm—50 (54–60) sts. Join A and work around in stockinette st for 3 rnds.

For size 4 only: Follow Chart 5, repeat from A to B around.

For size 6 only: Follow Chart 6, repeat from A to B around 5 times, ending at C.

For size 8 only: Follow Chart 6, repeat from A to B around.
Continue as established until sleeve measures 7¾″ (8¾″–9¾″) from underarm or desired length, dec 14 sts evenly spaced across last rnd—36 (40–46) sts. Change to No. 4 dp needles. Work in ribbing of k 1, p 1 for 2¼″. Bind off in ribbing.

FINISHING: Sew underarm seams tog.

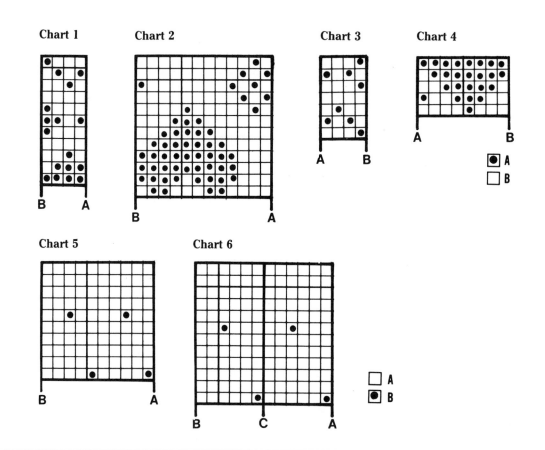

Chart 1 Chart 2 Chart 3 Chart 4

⊡ A
☐ B

Chart 5 Chart 6

☐ A
⊡ B

PART II
KNITTED ACCESSORIES AND TOYS

Here are hats and mittens in adult and children's sizes, plus slipper socks, golf club socks, an afghan, and some dolls, projects that make wonderful gifts for young or old.

For added amusement, the dolls turn from storybook characters into the animals associated with them; for example, Goldilocks, upside down, becomes a baby bear.

Head-to-Toe Accessories with Bobbles, Cables, or Stripes

From club socks to slipper socks, mittens, hats, and a scarf, there is something in this woolly array to satisfy almost anyone of any age, especially at Christmas.

Striped Club Covers

MATERIALS: Knitting worsted weight yarn, 4 ozs. natural (MC), 2 ozs. rust (CC). Knitting needles, No. 8 (5½ mm). Crochet hook, size H (5 mm).

GAUGE: 9 sts = 2″; 11 rows = 2 ″.

SOCK 1: Cast on 34 sts. Work in k 2, p 2 ribbing for 5″.

Next Row (right side): K 2 tog, * p 2 tog, k 2 tog; repeat from * across—17 sts. Work in k 1, p 1 ribbing for 3 rows.

Inc Row: Inc 1 st in each st across—34 sts. P 1 row. Work in stockinette st (k 1 row, p 1 row), working 8 rows more of MC, 3 rows CC, 9 rows MC.

Dec Row 1: With MC, * k 2 tog; repeat from * across—17 sts.

Dec Row 2: * K 2 tog; repeat from * across, end k 1—9 sts. Break yarn, leaving a 12″ end. Thread end in yarn needle and draw through sts, slipping sts from needle. Draw up sts tightly and fasten securely. Sew side seam.

SOCK 2: Work same as sock 1 through Inc Row—34 sts. P 1 row. In stockinette st, work 6 rows more MC, 3 rows CC, 4 rows MC, 3 rows CC, 4 rows MC. With MC, work dec rows and finish same as sock 1.

SOCK 3: Work same as sock 1 through Inc Row—34 sts. P 1 row. In stockinette st, work 3 rows more MC, 3 rows CC, 3 rows MC, 3 rows CC, 3 rows MC, 3 rows CC, 2 rows MC. With MC, work dec rows and finish same as sock 1.

SOCK 4: Work same as sock 1 through Inc Row—34 sts. P 1 row. In stockinette st, * work 3 rows CC, 2 rows MC; repeat from * 3 times more. With MC, work dec rows and finish same as sock 1.

POMPOMS (make 4): Holding 1 strand each of MC and CC tog as 1, wind yarn around a 1½″ piece of cardboard about 150 times. Tie very tightly at one end, cut opposite end. Roll in palm of hand to form ball; trim evenly. Attach 1 pompom to top of each sock.

LINKING CORD: With size H hook and 1 strand each of MC and CC, join with sl st to 1 st in first dec row at top of Sock 1, ch 24, join with sl st to 1 st in first dec row at top of Sock 2, ch 24, join to Sock 3 as for Sock 2, ch 24, join to Sock 4 as for Sock 2. Fasten off.

Cabled Club Covers

MATERIALS: Knitting worsted weight yarn, 5 ozs. of MC, 3 yds. of CC for numbers. Knitting needles, Nos. 4 (3½ mm) and 6 (4½ mm). Crochet hook, size H (5 mm). Cable needle. Four ½″ plastic rings. Macrame cord, 15″ length.

GAUGE: Stockinette st, No. 6 needles, 5 sts = 1″; 13 rows = 2″.

COVERS (make 4): With No. 4 needles, cast on 36 sts. Work in k 2, p 2 ribbing for 5″.

Inc Row: Working in ribbing, inc 1 st in every 3rd st 11 times—47 sts.

PATTERN

Row 1 (right side): * (K 1, p 1) twice, sk next st, k in front lp of next st leaving st on needle, k in front lp of skipped st, sl both sts from needle (twist st), twist st over next 2 sts, p 1, k 1, p 2, k 6, p 2, k 1, p 1, (twist st) twice, p 1, k 1, p 1 *, place marker on needle, (k 1, p 7) twice, k 1, p 1. Carry markers.

Row 2 and all even rows: K all k sts, p all p sts.

Row 3: * K 1, p 1, k in front, back, front, back, and front of next st then pass first 4 sts over last st (bobble), p 1, (twist st) twice, p 1, bobble, p 2, sl next 3 sts to cable needle and hold in back of work, k next 3 sts, k 3 sts from cable needle (cable twist), p 2, bobble, p 1, (twist st) twice, p 1, bobble, p 1 *, k 1, p 6, k 3, p 6, k 1, p 1.

Row 5: Repeat between *'s of row 1 once, k 1, p 5, k 5, p 5, k 1, p 1.

Row 7: * K 1, p 1, bobble, p 1, (twist st) twice, p 1, bobble, p 2, k 6, p 2, bobble, p 1, (twist st) twice, p 1, bobble, p 1 *, k 1, p 4, k 7, p 4, k 1, p 1.

Row 9: * (K 1, p 1) twice, (twist st) twice, p 1, k 1, p 2, cable twist, p 2, k 1, p 1, (twist st) twice, p 1, k 1, p 1 *, k 1, p 3, k 9, p 3, k 1, p 1.

Row 11: Repeat between *'s of row 7 once, k 1, p 2, k 11, p 2, k 1, p 1.

Row 13: Repeat between *'s of row 1 once, k 1, p 1, k 13, p 1, k 1, p 1.

Row 15: Repeat between *'s of row 3 once, k 1, p 2, k 11, p 2, k 1, p 1.

Row 17: Repeat between *'s of row 1 once, k 1, p 3, k 9, p 3, k 1, p 1.

Row 19: Repeat between *'s of row 7 once, k 1, p 4, k 7, p 4, k 1, p 1.

Row 21: Repeat between *'s of row 9 once, k 1, p 5, k 5, p 5, k 1, p 1.

Row 23: Repeat between *'s of row 7 once, k 1, p 6, k 3, p 6, k 1, p 1.

Row 25: Repeat row 1.

Row 27: (K 2 tog) 4 times, p 1, k 1, p 2, (k 2 tog) 3 times, p 2, k 1, p 1, (k 2 tog) 3 times, p 1, k 1, (p 2 tog) 3 times, p 1, k 1, p 1, (p 2 tog) 3 times, k 1, p 1—31 sts.

Row 28: K 1, (p 1, k 4) twice, p 1, k 1, p 3, k 1, p 1, k 2, p 3, k 2, p 1, k 1, p 4.

Row 29: (K 2 tog) 3 times, p 2 tog, sl 1, k 2 tog, psso, (p 2 tog) twice, k 2 tog, p 2 tog, k 1, (p 2 tog) twice, k 1, (p 2 tog) 3 times—16 sts.

Row 30: * P 2 tog; repeat from * across—8 sts.

FINISHING: Break yarn, leaving a 12″ end. Thread end in yarn needle and draw through sts, slipping sts from needle. Draw up sts tightly and fasten securely. Sew side seam.

POMPOMS (make 4): Wind yarn around a 1½″ piece of cardboard about 300 times, tie very tightly at one end, cut opposite end. Roll in palm of hand to form ball, trim ends evenly. Attach 1 pompom to top of each cover.

NUMBERS: With size H hook and CC, leaving a 10″ end at beg for sewing, make a ch about 4″ long for each of the 4 numbers. Fasten off, leaving end for adjusting. On the stockinette st diamond of each cover, form a number 1, 3, 4 and a 2 or 5 (golfer's preference). Pin in place and sew, adding or removing chs as needed. Sew 1 ring under each pompom. Thread cord through rings and knot securely.

Child's Cap and Mittens

SIZE: One cap size fits all. Mittens, 6–10 years.

MATERIALS: Knitting worsted weight yarn, 5 ozs. Knitting needles, Nos. 6 and 8 (4½ mm and 5½ mm). 1 cable needle.

GAUGE: Stockinette st: 4 sts = 1″; 6 rows = 1″

CAP: With No. 6 needles, cast on 85 sts. Work in k 1, p 1 ribbing for 14 rows, inc 7 sts evenly spaced in last row—92 sts. Change to No. 8 needles.

PATTERN

Row 1 (right side): * K 2, p 3, k 6, p 1, k 2, p 2, sk next st, k in back lp of next st leaving st on needle, then k skipped st in front lp, sl both sts from needle (twist st), p 1, k in front, back, front, back, and front of next st and sl first 4 sts over last st (popcorn), p 1, twist st, repeat from * across.

Row 2 and All Even Rows: K all k sts and p all p sts.

Row 3: * P 2, k 2, p 1, sl next 3 sts to cable needle, hold in front of work, k next 3 sts, k 3 sts from cable needle (cable twist), p 3, k 2, twist st, p 3, twist st, repeat from * across.

Row 5: Repeat row 1.

Row 7: * P 2, k 2, p 1, k 6, p 3, k 2, twist st, p 3, twist st; repeat from * across.

Row 9: * K 2, p 3, cable twist, p 1, k 2, p 2, twist st, p 1, popcorn, p 1, twist st; repeat from * across.

Row 11: Repeat row 7.

Row 12: Repeat row 2. Repeat rows 1–12 once more, then repeat rows 1–6 once.

Next Row: * K 2 tog; repeat from * across— 46 sts. P 1 row. Repeat last 2 rows 3 times more—6 sts. Break yarn, leaving a 15″ end.

FINISHING: Thread end in yarn needle and draw through sts, sl sts from needle. Draw sts up tightly and fasten securely. Sew back seam.

POMPOM: Wind yarn around a 2″ piece of cardboard about 300 times. Tie very tightly at one end, cut opposite end. Roll in palm of hand to form ball. Trim ends evenly. Attach pompom to top of cap.

MITTENS

RIGHT HAND: With No. 6 needles, cast on 28 sts. Work in k 1, p 1 ribbing for 20 rows, inc 7 sts evenly spaced in last row—35 sts. Change to No. 8 needles.

Row 1: K 3, place marker on needle, k 2, p 1, sl next 3 sts to cable needle and hold in front, k next 3 sts, k 3 sts from cable needle (cable twist), p 1, k 2, place marker on needle, k 20. Carry markers.

Row 2 and All Even Rows: P all p sts, k all k sts.

Row 3: K 3, p 3, k 6, p 3, k 20.

Thumb Gusset

Row 5: K 5, p 1, k 6, p 1, k 2, k 1, place marker on needle for gusset, inc 1 st in next st, k 1, inc 1 st in next st, place marker for gusset, k 16—37 sts. Carry all markers.

Row 7: K 3, p 3, cable twist, p 3, * k to next marker, inc 1 st in next st, k to within 1 st of next marker, inc 1 st in next st, k to end *—39 sts.

Row 9: K 3, k 2, p 1, k 6, p 1, k 2; repeat between *'s of row 7 once—41 sts.

Row 11: K 3, p 3, k 6, p 3; repeat between *'s of row 7 once—43 sts.

Row 13: K 3, p 3, cable twist, p 3, k 1; dropping gusset markers, sl next 11 sts to holder for thumb, cast on 2 sts, k to end—34 sts.

Hand: Working pat between markers as established in rows 1–12 and remaining sts in stockinette st, work even until 4½″ above ribbing or 1½″ less than desired length to fingertips, end with wrong side row.

Next Row: Keeping pat, * k 1, k 2 tog, repeat from * across. P 1 row. Repeat last 2 rows

twice—11 sts. Break yarn, leaving a 12″ end. Thread end in yarn needle and draw through sts, sl sts from needle. Draw sts up tightly and fasten securely. Do not cut yarn.

Thumb: With right side facing, sl 11 sts to size 8 needle, cast on 1 st at beg, k across, cast on 1 st at end—13 sts. P 1 row. Work in stockinette st for 1½″.

Next Row: * K 2 tog, repeat from * across— 6 sts. P 1 row. Repeat last 2 rows once—3 sts. Break yarn, leaving a 6″ end. Finish as for top of mitten, sew seam. Sew side seam of mitten.

LEFT HAND: Work ribbing same as right mitten. Change to No. 8 needles.

Row 1: K 20, place marker on needle, k 2, p 1, cable twist, p 1, k 2, place marker, k 3. Finish as for right mitten, reversing shaping.

Adult Mittens

SIZE: Women's size.

MATERIALS: Knitting worsted, 2 ozs. Knitting needles, No. 8. Dp needle.

GAUGE: 4 sts = 1″.

RIGHT MITTEN: Cast on 36 sts, work in k 1, p 1 ribbing for 4″.

PATTERN

Row 1: K 4, p 2, * sl next 2 sts as if to p on a dp needle, hold in back, k next 2 sts, then k sts from dp needle, sl next 2 sts on a dp needle, hold in front, k next 2 sts, then k sts from dp needle, * p 2, k to end of row.

Row 2: P 20, k 2, p 8, k 2, p 4.

Row 3: K 4, p 2, k 8, p 2, k 2, inc 1 st in next st (thumb inc), k 1, inc 1 st in next st (thumb inc), k to end.

Row 4: P 22, k 2, p 8, k 2, p 4.

Row 5: K 4, p 2, k 8, p 2, k 2, inc 1 st in next st, k 3, inc 1 st in next st, k to end.

Row 6: P the p sts, k the k sts.

Row 7: K 4, p 2, work from * to * of row 1 for

cable, p 2, k 2, inc 1 st in next st, k 5, inc 1 st in next st, k to end.

Row 8: Repeat row 6.

Row 9: K 4, p 2, k 8, p 2, k 2, inc 1 st in next st, k 7, inc 1 st in next st, k to end.

Row 10: Repeat row 6.

Row 11: K 4, p 2, k 8, p 2, k 2, inc 1 st in next st, k 9, inc 1 st in next st, k to end.

Row 12: Repeat row 6.

Row 13: K 4, p 2, work from * to * of row 1 for cable, p 2, k 2; sl next 13 sts to a holder; cast on 3 sts; k to end.

Row 14: Repeat row 6.

Row 15: K 4, p 2, k 8, p 2, k to end. Repeat last 2 rows, working cable twist every 6th row, until 7 cable twists have been made or until mitten is 1″ less than desired length, end wrong side.

Shape Top

Row 1: K 1, sl 1, k 1, psso, k 1, p 2, k 8, p 2, k 1, k 2 tog, k 1, sl 1, k 1, psso, k to last 3 sts, k 2 tog, k 1.

Row 2: P the p sts, k the k sts.

Row 3: K 1, sl 1, k 1, psso, p 2 tog, sl 1, k 1, psso, k 4, k 2 tog, p 2 tog, k 2 tog, sl 1, k 1, psso, k 1, sl 1, k 1, psso, k 4, (k 2 tog, k 1) twice.

Row 4: Repeat row 2.

Row 5: * K 1, k 2 tog, repeat from * across, end k 1. Cut yarn, leaving long end. Run through remaining sts, gather in sts slightly, sew top seam. Sew side seam after thumb is completed.

Thumb: Pick up and k 3 sts on cast-on sts at thumb, k across thumb sts. Work even on thumb sts for 1½″, end p row.

Next Row: * K 1, k 2 tog, repeat from * across, end k 1, P 1 row.

Next Row: * K 2 tog, k 1, repeat from * across. Cut yarn, leaving end for sewing. Run through remaining sts, draw sts tog tightly; sew thumb seam.

LEFT MITTEN: Work as for right mitten through ribbing.

PATTERN

Row 1: K 20, p 2, work cable pat on next 8 sts, p 2, k 4. Finish as for right mitten, reversing shaping.

Slipper Socks

SIZE: Socks will fit 8″–10″ foot.

MATERIALS: Knitting worsted weight yarn, 1 3½-oz. skein for calf length, 2 skeins for knee length. Knitting needles, No. 8 (5 mm). 1 cable needle.

GAUGE: 9 sts = 2″; 6 rows = 1″

FOOT: Cast on 76 sts. K 1 row.

Row 2: K 38, place marker on needle, k to end. Carry marker.

Row 3: * K 1, inc 1 st in next st, k to within 2 sts of marker, inc 1 st in next st, k 1; repeat from * once making last inc 1 st from end—80 sts. K 1 row. Repeat last 2 rows twice more—88 sts. Work even in garter st (k each row) for 14 rows more—11 ridges each side.

Shape Instep

Row 1: K to within 5 sts of marker, p 2, k 6, p 2 (last 10 sts form cable panel), k 2 tog. Turn. Drop marker.

Rows 2, 4, 6 and 8: Sl 1, k 2, p 6, k 2, k 2 tog. Turn.

Row 3: Sl 1, p 2, sl next 3 sts to cable needle and hold in back, k next 3 sts, k 3 sts from cable needle (cable twist), p 2, k 2 tog. Turn.

Rows 5 and 7: Sl 1, p 2, k 6, p 2, k 2 tog. Turn. Repeat rows 3–8, 3 times more, then rows 3 and 4 once more—60 sts.

Next Row: Sl 1, p 2, k 6, p 2, k to end.

Next Row: (P 1, k 1) 5 times, * p 1, k 1 (p 2, k 1) twice, p 1 *, k 8, p 6, k 8; repeat between *'s once, (k 1, p 1) 5 times.

LEG

Row 1: (K 1, p 1) 6 times, sk next st, k in front lp of next st leaving st on needle, then k in front lp of skipped st, sl both sts from needle (twist st), p 1, twist st, p 1, k 1, p 2, p 2 tog, p 4, cable twist, p 4, p 2 tog, p 2, k 1, (p 1, twist st) twice, (p 1, k 1) 6 times—58 sts.

Row 2: (P 1, k 1) 5 times, * p 1, (k 1, p 2) twice, k 1, p 1 *, k 7, p 6, k 7; repeat between *'s once, (k 1, p 1) 5 times.

Row 3: (K 1, p 1) 5 times, * k in front, back, front, and back of next st and sl first 3 sts over last st (popcorn), (p 1, twist st) twice, p 1, popcorn *, p 2, p 2 tog, p 3, k 6, p 3, p 2 tog, p 1; repeat between *'s once, (p 1, k 1) 5 times—56 sts.

Row 4: (P 1, k 1) 5 times, * p 1, (k 1, p 2) twice, k 1, p 1 *, k 6, p 6, k 6; repeat between *'s once, (k 1, p 1) 5 times.

Row 5: (K 1, p 1) 5 times, * k 1, (p 1, twist st) twice, p 1, k 1 *, p 1, p 2 tog, p 3, k 6, p 3, p 2 tog, p 1; repeat between *'s once, (p 1, k 1) 5 times—54 sts.

Row 6: (P 1, k 1) 5 times, * p 1, (k 1, p 2) twice, k 1, p 1 *, place marker on needle, k 5, p 6, k 5, place marker on needle; repeat between *'s once, (k 1, p 1) 5 times. Continue in pat, repeat rows 3–6 for sts outside markers, and work established cable twist and reverse stockinette st over sts between markers, until 1″ less than desired length, end with right side row. Drop markers.

Next Row: (P 1, k 1) 13 times, p 2 tog, (k 1, p 1) 13 times. Work in k 1, p 1 ribbing for 1″. Bind off loosely in ribbing.

FINISHING: Break yarn, leaving a 24″ end. Sew back and foot seam.

Matching Scarf, Hat, and Mittens

SIZE: One size fits all.

MATERIALS: Knitting worsted weight yarn, 4 4-oz. skeins. Susan Bates or Marcia Lynn 16″ circular knitting needle No. 9. Set of double-pointed needles, No. 9. Susan Bates "Trim-Tool"™ for fringe.

GAUGE: 9 sts = 2″; 7 rows = 1″

PATTERN

Row 1 (wrong side): Purl.

Row 2: Knit.

Row 3: P 1, * p 1 wrapping yarn twice around needle, p 2, p 1 wrapping yarn twice, p 1; repeat from * across.

Row 4: K 1, * sl 1 dropping 2nd wrap, k 2, sl 1 dropping 2nd wrap, k 1, yo, k 1, yo, k 1 all in next st; repeat from * across, end last repeat k 1.

Row 5: P 1, * sl 1, p 2, sl 1, k 5; repeat from * across, end last repeat p 1.

Row 6: K 1, * sl 1, k 2, p 5; repeat from * across, end last repeat k 1.

Row 7: P 1, * sl 1, p 2, sl 1, k 2 tog, k 3 tog, pass k 2 tog st over k 3 tog st; repeat from * across, end last repeat p 1.

Row 8: K 1, * drop first long st off needle to front, sl next 2 sts, drop next long st off needle to front, pick up first long lp and sl back to left needle, sl 2 sl sts back to left needle, pick up 2nd long lp and sl back to left needle, k 5; repeat from * across. Repeat rows 1–8 for pat.

Note: When working pat in rnds for hat and mittens, k all p sts on odd rows, and, in row 5, work k 5 as p 5; in row 7, work k 2 tog, k 3 tog as p 2 tog, p 3 tog. As decs and pat beg, sl sts to preceding or following needle as necessary.

SCARF: With circular needle, cast on 40 sts. Do not join, work back and forth in rows. K 1 row.

Next Row (right side): K 12, place marker on needle, work pat row 2 across next 16 sts, place marker on needle, k 12.

Next Row: K 4 for garter st edge, p 8, sl marker, work pat row 3 to next marker, sl marker, p 8, k 4 for garter st edge. (**Note:** Carry markers throughout.)

Working pat between markers, repeat last 2

rows for side sts. Work even until 60" from beg, end with right side row. K 1 row. Bind off.

Fringe: With Trim-Tool™, cut 7" fringe lengths. Using 2 strands for each fringe, knot a fringe in every other st across each short end.

HAT: With dp needles, cast on 80 sts. Divide sts on 3 needles as follows: 22 sts on first needle, 20 sts on 2nd needle, 38 sts on 3rd needle.

Rnd 1: With care not to twist sts, join, * k 4, place marker on needle, work in pat across next 16 sts (see pat note for working in rnds), repeat from * around—4 k panels, 4 pat panels. Carry markers. Repeat rnd 1 until 1½" from beg.

Next rnd: * K 1, k 2 tog, k 1, work in pat across next 16 sts; repeat from * around—76 sts. Work even in pat as established until 4" from beg, end with pat row 8. Work 2 rnds more, replacing old markers with a marker on center st of k panels.

Next rnd: Work around, dec 1 st each side of each marked st and working only the center 6 sts of each pat panel in pat, k remaining sts—68 sts.

Next rnd: Work even. Repeat last 2 rnds 3 times more, discontinuing pat after 2nd dec rnd—44 sts.

Next rnd: Dec 1 st each side of each marked st and 2 sts across 6-st panel—28 sts. K 1 rnd.

Next rnd: * K 2 tog; repeat from * around—14 sts. Cut yarn, leaving a 6" end. Thread end in tapestry needle, draw through sts and sl from needle. Draw up tightly and fasten securely.

BRIM: From right side, with circular needle, pick up and k 80 sts along cast-on edge. Join and k 2 rnds. Inc 10 sts evenly spaced in next rnd, then every 3rd rnd 6 times more—150 sts. K 2 rnds. P 1 rnd for turning ridge. K 2

rnds. Dec 10 sts evenly spaced in next rnd, then every 3rd rnd 6 times more—80 sts. K 2 rnds. Bind off. Fold brim to wrong side along ridge. Sew in place with care not to pull sts too tight.

MITTENS

RIGHT HAND: With dp needles, cast on 36 sts. Divide evenly on 3 needles. With care not to twist sts, join and work around in k 1, p 1 ribbing for 5 rnds, dec 6 sts evenly spaced in last rnd—30 sts. Work in pat for 16 rnds, omitting first st (work only the sts following the *). See pat note for working in rnds. K 4 rnds.

Shape Thumb: K 4, place marker on needle, inc 1 st in each of next 2 sts, place marker on needle, k to end. K 3 rnds even. Carry markers.

Next rnd: K to marker, inc 1 st in next st, k to within 1 st of next marker, inc 1 st in next st, k to end. Repeat last 4 rnds 3 times more—12 sts between markers; 40 sts. K 1 rnd.

Next rnd: K to marker, sl next 12 sts to holder, cast on 2 sts, k to end—30 sts. Work even until 1½" less than desired length to fingertips.

Shape Top

Next rnd: * K 2 tog, k 4; repeat from * around. K 1 rnd. Repeat last 2 rnds, having 1 less st between decs in each successive rnd, until 10 sts remain. Break yarn, leaving a 6" end. Thread end in tapestry needle, draw through sts and sl from needle. Draw up tightly and fasten securely.

Thumb: Sl 12 sts to 3 needles. Join yarn at inside edge and pick up 1 st in each of the 2 cast-on sts of hand—14 sts. K 1 rnd, dec 1 st at each inside corner—12 sts. Work even until thumb measures desired finished length. K 2 tog all around. Finish same as top.

Left hand: Work same as right mitten.

Stars-and-Bars Afghan

With its bold red, white, and blue color scheme, this eye-catching afghan has both a patriotic as well as a nautical look. It would be particularly handsome in a young boy's room or in a country-style setting. It is made in four panels that are worked in stockinette stitch and finished with a crocheted border.

SIZE: 50″ × 56″

MATERIALS: Knitting worsted, 7 4-oz. skeins white, 4 skeins blue, 3 skeins red. Knitting needles, No. 7. Steel crochet hook No. 0. Set of bobbins.

GAUGE: 5 sts = 1 ″; 6 rows = 1″

STRIPS (make 4): With blue, cast on 61 sts. P 1 row. Following chart, beg with row 1 (bottom row has already been worked), work in stockinette st (k 1 row, p 1 row) to top of chart. Use a bobbin for each separate color section. In center section, white can be carried across back of stars.

Repeat from row 1 to top of chart until 6 blocks have been completed.

FINISHING: Weave in ends on wrong side. Sew strips tog.

EDGING

Rnd 1: Join blue in edge of afghan. Sc in 2 sts, * sk 1 st, sc in next 2 sts, repeat from * around, working sc, ch 1, sc in each corner. Join with sl st in first sc.

Rnd 2: Ch 3, dc in st before ch 3, * sk next st, dc in next st, dc in skipped st (cross st made), repeat from * around, working ch 3 between cross sts at corners. Join with sl st in top of ch 3.

Rnd 3: Ch 1, sk first st, sc in next dc, sc in skipped st, * sk next dc, sc in next dc, sc in skipped dc, repeat from * around, working 2 sc, ch 1, 2 sc in each corner sp. Join. End off.

Block afghan using damp cloth and lukewarm iron.

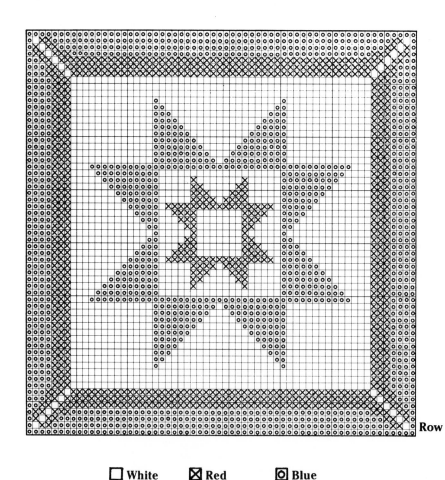

Row 1

☐ White   ☒ Red   ⊙ Blue

Storybook Topsy-turvy Dolls

Though you may not recognize Cinderella, Dorothy, Goldilocks, and Alice at first, their identity becomes clear once they are turned upside-down to reveal Fairy Godmother, Cowardly Lion, Baby Bear, and White Rabbit. Their bodies are knitted in garter stitch, and the skirts are crocheted.

Dorothy and the Cowardly Lion

SIZE: About 10″ tall

MATERIALS: Knitting worsted weight yarn: 3 ozs. turquoise, 1 oz. each light pink, brown, and dark gold. Red embroidery floss. Polyester filling. Knitting needles, No. 4. Crochet hook, size D. Tapestry needle.

GAUGE: 4 sts = 1″.

Notes: Dolls are knitted in garter st (k each row). When changing colors, always tie in colors at same side of work; leave 12″ end for sewing doll tog.

DOROTHY: Beg at waist, with turquoise, cast on 10 sts. K 16 rows. Cut turquoise, tie in pink. With pink, k 12 rows. Cut pink, tie in brown. With brown, k 24 rows. Cut brown, tie in turquoise. With turquoise, k 16 rows. Cut turquoise, tie in gold.

LION: With gold, k 68 rows. Bind off.

Dorothy's Arms (make 2): With pink, cast on 8 sts. K 4 rows. Cut pink, tie in turquoise. With turquoise, k 14 rows. Bind off.

Lion's Arms (make 2): With gold, cast on 8 sts. K 18 rows. Bind off.

Lion's Ears and Snout (make 3 pieces): With gold, ch 2; 4 sc in 2nd ch from hook, sl st in first sc. Ch 1, turn. Work 2 sc in each sc around. Sl st in first sc. End off.

Dorothy's Skirt: With turquoise, ch 23.

Row 1: Sc in 2nd ch from hook and in each ch across—22 sc. Ch 3, turn.

Row 2: Dc in first sc, 2 dc in each sc across—44 dc. Ch 3, turn.

Row 3: Dc in first dc, dc in next dc, * 2 dc in next dc, dc in each of next 2 dc, repeat from * across, end dc in top of turning ch. Ch 3, turn.

Row 4: Dc in first dc, dc in next dc, * 2 dc in next dc, dc in each of next 3 dc, repeat from * across, end dc in top of turning ch. Ch 3, turn.
    Work 9 more rows of dc, without increasing. End off.

FINISHING: Sew cast-on and bound-off edges tog. Sew up side edges on wrong side, rounding off corners slightly at each end to shape heads. Leave opening at one side of lion's body for turning and stuffing. Turn to right side; stuff firmly; sew up side. Gather top row of Dorothy's blouse with matching yarn to form neck. Fasten yarn securely. With gold yarn, indent lion's neck in same way.
    Fold arms lengthwise, sew up hands and sides; leave top open. Stuff and sew to sides of body ¼″ below neck. Pull arms slightly toward front and catch to front of body. Finish lion's arms the same.

Dorothy's Hair: For each braid, cut 12 7″ lengths of brown yarn, tie strands firmly tog at center. Fold strands at tie and braid ends for 1¼″ below tie. Fasten securely. Sew top of braid to hairline, sew braid to side of face. Tie yarn bows around braids. Embroider bangs in straight sts across forehead. (See *Embroidery Stitches* section at back of book.)

Dorothy's Face: With red floss, embroider tiny mouth in straight st. With black yarn or floss, embroider 1 lazy daisy st for each eye.

Lion's Mane: Using doubled brown yarn and a tapestry needle and working around oval of face, pull strand of yarn through knitted st leaving 1″ loop; take a small st through same st to fasten loop. Cut through loops; trim mane.

Lion's Face: Sew ears below mane at top of face. Sew snout to lower center of face. With brown yarn and satin stitches, embroider nose triangle. Embroider eyes as for Dorothy.

Dorothy's Skirt: Place skirt on doll; sew up back seam. Sew skirt to doll at waistline.

Goldilocks and the Bear

MATERIALS: Knitting worsted weight yarn, 3 ozs. red, 2 ozs. brown, 1 oz. each of yellow and pink. Polyester filling. Knitting needles, No. 4. Crochet hook, size D. Tapestry needle. Embroidery floss: red, blue, and pink.

GAUGE: 4 sts = 1″

GOLDILOCKS: Beg at waist, with red, cast on 10 sts. K 16 rows. Cut red, tie in pink. With pink, k 12 rows. Cut pink, tie in yellow. With yellow, k 24 rows. Cut yellow, tie in red. With red, k 16 rows. Cut red, tie in brown.

BEAR: With brown, k 68 rows. Bind off.

Goldilocks' Arms (make 2): With pink, cast on 8 sts. K 4 rows. Cut pink, tie in red. With red, k 14 rows. Bind off.

Bear's Arms (make 2): With brown, cast on 8 sts. K 18 rows. Bind off.

Bear's Ears and Snout (make 3 pieces): With brown, work as for Lion's ears and snout.

Goldilock's Skirt: With red, work as for Dorothy's skirt through Row 4. At end of Row 4, sl st in top of ch 3 at beg of row to join work. Ch 3; do not turn. Work 9 rnds of dc from right side without increasing, sl st in top of ch 3 to join each rnd. End off.

FINISHING: Sew up and stuff doll as for Dorothy and Lion.

Goldilocks' Hair: Cut 10 3″ strands of yellow for each tuft. Tie strands tog at center with matching yarn. Sew a tuft to each side of head at hairline. Tie red yarn bows to hair.

Goldilocks' Face: With red floss, embroider small mouth in straight st. With blue yarn or floss, embroider eyes in lazy daisy st.

Bear's Face: Sew ears to top of head. Sew snout to lower center of face. With pink floss and satin stitches, embroider nose triangle. Embroider eyes as for Goldilocks.

Goldilock's Skirt: Place skirt on doll. Sew up back opening. Sew skirt to doll at waistline.

Alice and the White Rabbit

MATERIALS: Knitting worsted weight yarn, 3 ozs. purple, 2 ozs. white, 1 oz. each pink and yellow. Polyester filling. Knitting needles, No. 4. Crochet hook, size D. Yarn needle.

GAUGE: 4 sts = 1″

ALICE: Beg at waist, with purple, cast on 10 sts. K 16 rows. Cut purple, tie in pink. With pink, k 12 rows. Cut pink, tie in yellow. With yellow k 24 rows. Cut yellow, tie in purple. With purple, k 16 rows. Cut purple, tie in white.

RABBIT: With white, k 68 rows. Bind off.

Alice's Arms (make 2): With pink, cast on 8 sts. K 4 rows. Cut pink, tie in purple. With purple, k 14 rows. Bind off.

Rabbit's Arms (make 2): With white, cast on 8 sts. K 18 rows. Bind off.

Rabbit's Ears (make 2): With white, ch 5.

Row 1: Sc in 2nd ch from hook and in each of next 3 ch. Ch 1, turn.

Rows 2–5: Sc in each sc. Ch 1, turn each row.

Row 6: Sc in first st; pull up a lp in each of next 2 sts, yo and through 3 lps on hook, sc in last sc. Ch 1, turn.

Row 7: Pull up a lp in each of first and 2nd sts, yo and through 3 lps on hook, sc in last sc. Ch 1, turn.

Row 8: Dec as before over last 2 sc. End off.

Alice's Skirt: With purple, work as for Dorothy's skirt, making rows 8 and 10 in white.

FINISHING: Sew up and stuff doll as for Dorothy and Lion.

Alice's Hair: Wind yellow yarn around 2″-wide piece of cardboard 8 times. Tie strands tightly tog at one edge; cut through strands at opposite edge. Sew tied ends to side of head at hairline. Trim hair with bows.

Alice's Face: With red, embroider small mouth in straight st. With blue yarn or floss, embroider eyes in lazy daisy st.

Rabbit's Face: Sew ears to head. With pink yarn or floss and satin stitches, embroider triangle for nose. Make eyes as for Alice's eyes.

Alice's Skirt: Place skirt on doll; sew up back seam. Sew skirt to doll at waistline.

Cinderella and Her Fairy Godmother

MATERIALS: Knitting worsted weight yarn, 3 ozs. yellow, 1 oz. each brown, pink, and dark gold. Red embroidery floss. Polyester filling. Knitting needles, No. 4. Crochet hook, size D. Tapestry needle. 5″ sequin braid.

GAUGE: 4 sts = 1″

FAIRY GODMOTHER: Beg at waist, with yellow, cast on 10 sts. K 16 rows. Cut yellow, tie in pink. With pink, k 12 rows. Cut pink, tie in brown. With brown, k 24 rows. Cut brown, tie in yellow. With yellow, k 16 rows. Cut yellow, tie in brown.

CINDERELLA: With brown, k 16 rows. Cut brown, tie in yellow. With yellow, k 24 rows. Cut yellow, tie in pink. With pink, k 12 rows. Cut pink, tie in brown. With brown, k 16 rows. Bind off.

Fairy Godmother's Arms (make 2): With pink cast on 8 sts. K 4 rows. Cut pink, tie in yellow. With yellow, k 14 rows. Bind off.

Cinderella's Arms: Work as for Fairy Godmother's arms, using brown instead of yellow.

Skirt: With yellow, ch 23.

Row 1: Sc in 2nd ch from hook and in each ch across—22 sc. Ch 3, turn.

Row 2: Dc in first sc, 2 dc in each sc across—44 dc. Ch 3, turn.

Row 3: Dc in first dc, dc in next dc, * 2 dc in next dc, dc in each of next 2 dc, repeat from * across, end dc in top of turning ch. Ch 3, turn.

Row 4: Dc in first dc, dc in next dc, * 2 dc in next dc, dc in each of next 3 dc, repeat from * across, end dc in top of turning ch. Sl st in top of ch 3 at beg of row to join work. Ch 3; do not turn. Work 9 rnds of dc without increasing, sl st in top of ch 3 to join each rnd. End off.

Apron: With gold, ch 7.

Row 1: Sc in 2nd ch from hook and in each remaining ch—6 sc. Ch 3, turn each row.

Row 2: 2 dc in each sc across.

Row 3: * Dc in each of next 2 dc, 2 dc in next dc, repeat from * across.

Row 4: * Dc in each of 3 dc, 2 dc in next dc, repeat from * across. Work 3 more rows of dc without increasing. End off.

Make 2 gold chains about 6″ long. Sew to top ends of apron for ties.

FINISHING: Sew up and stuff doll as for Dorothy and Lion.

Cinderella's Hair: Same as Alice's hair. Tack hair ends tog at sides of face.

Cinderella's Face: Same as Alice's face.

Fairy Godmother's Face: Same as Alice's face.

Fairy Godmother's Hair: With brown, embroider lazy daisy sts all around face. Form crown from sequin braid, sew to head.

Skirt: Place skirt on doll; sew up back seam. Sew skirt to doll at waistline. Sew apron to front of skirt on Cinderella side. Tie ends at back.

PART III

CROCHET FOR ALL AGES

From colorful infant's clothing to a sophisticated tunic, the designs in this section were chosen to meet the needs of children as well as adults. The selection for children includes an infant's suit with matching accessories, summer outfits for little girls, and winter sweaters for both sexes. For women, the choice of sweaters ranges from lacy summer cardigans to pullovers for different seasons

Lacy Cardigans That Are Made for Each Other

Wearing two cardigans, especially in summer, is a bit unusual, but this airy pair is not only smartly cool, but extremely practical. Worked in different but complementary patterns, the sweaters look great together, but they also provide versatility separately because one is sleeveless.

SIZES: Directions are for small size (8–10). Changes for medium size (12–14) are in parentheses.

Note: Size of hook and gauge determine size.

Body Bust Size: 31½"–32½" (34"–36")

Blocked Bust Size: Cardigan, 35" (37"); **Sleeveless Sweater,** 35" (37").

MATERIALS: Fingering yarn, 10 (11) 1½ oz. balls for cardigan: 4 (5) balls for sleeveless sweater. Aluminum crochet hooks, sizes C and E (C and F). Five buttons.

GAUGE

Cardigan: 3 V sts and 2 shells = 3", size E hook (3¼", size F hook).

Sleeveless Sweater: 2 shells and 1 V st = 2", size E hook (2¼", size F hook).

Cardigan

Note: Body is worked in one piece to underarm.
  With E (F) hook, ch 173 loosely.

Row 1: Dc in 4th ch from hook (turning ch counts as 1 dc), * sk 2 ch; in next ch work 5 dc for a shell, sk 2 ch; in next ch work 1 dc, ch 1 and 1 dc for a V st; repeat from * to last 7 ch, sk 2 ch, 5-dc shell in next ch sk 2 ch, 1 dc in each of last 2 ch—28 shells, 27 V sts and 2 dc at each side. Ch 3, turn each row.

Row 2: Sk first dc (ch 3 counts as first dc), dc in next dc, dc in each of 5 dc of shell. * V st in ch-1 sp of next V st, dc in each of 5 dc of next shell, repeat from * across, end dc in each of last 2 dc.

Rows 3 and 4: Sk first dc, dc in each of next 6 dc, * V st in next V st, dc in each of next 5 dc, repeat from * across, end dc in each of last 2 dc. Piece should measure 35" (37") across.

Row 5: Sk first dc, dc in next dc, * sk 2 dc, V st in next dc, sk 2 dc, 5-dc shell in ch-1 sp of next V st, repeat from * across, end sk 2 dc, V st in next dc, sk 2 dc, dc in each of last 2 dc.

Row 6: Sk first dc, dc in next dc, 5 dc shell in ch-1 sp of next V st, * V st in 3rd dc of next shell, 5-dc shell in next V st, repeat from * across, end dc in each of last 2 dc.

Row 7: Sk first dc, dc in next dc, V st in 3rd dc of next shell, * shell in next V st, V st in 3rd dc of next shell, repeat from * across, end dc in each of last 2 dc.

Rows 8 and 9: Repeat Rows 6 and 7.

Row 10: Sk first dc, dc in next dc, V st in next V st, * dc in each of 5 dc of next shell, V st in next V st, repeat from * across, end dc in each of last 2 dc.

Rows 11 and 12: Sk first dc, dc in next dc, V st in next V st, * dc in each of next 5 dc, V st in next V st, repeat from * across, end dc in each of last 2 dc.

Row 13: Sk first dc, dc in next dc, shell in next V st, sk 2 dc, * V st in next dc, shell in next V st, repeat from * across, end dc in each of last 2 dc.

Row 14: Repeat Row 7.

Row 15: Repeat Row 13.

Rows 16 and 17: Repeat Rows 7 and 13. Repeat Rows 2–17 for pat working to about 14″ (15″) from beg, end with row 10.

Divide for Back and Fronts

RIGHT FRONT: Skip first dc, dc in next dc, * V st in next V st, dc in each of next 5 dc, repeat from * 5 more times end with dc in first dc of next V st. Ch 3, turn.

Continue in pat on right front sts until armhole measures 4½″ (5″) above underarm; end at armhole edge with row 9. Ch 3, turn.

Shape Neck and Shoulder: Sk first dc, * dc in each of next 5 dc, V st in next V st, repeat from * twice more. Ch 3, turn. Continue in pat until armhole measures 7″ (7½″) above underarm. End off.

LEFT FRONT: Join yarn in 7th V st from left front edge, ch 3 for first dc, work pat as on row 11 to front edge. Work to correspond to right front.

BACK: Leaving 1 shell, 1 V st and 1 shell free at right underarm, join yarn in 2nd st of next V st, work pat as on row 11 to left underarm, leaving 1 shell, 1 V st and 1 shell free for underarm. Ch 3, turn. Work in pat on back sts until armholes measure same as on fronts. Fasten off.

SLEEVES: With E (F) hook, ch 65 loosely. Work in pat same as on back with 10 shells, 11 V sts and 2 dc at each side. Work to about 16″ (17″) from start. End.

Cuffs (make 2): With C hook, ch 25.

Row 1: Sc in 2nd ch from hook and in each ch across—24 sc. Ch 1, turn.

Row 2: Working in back lps only, work sc in each sc. Ch 1, turn. Repeat row 2 to 7″ (8″) from beg. End off.

Front Bands (make 2): With C hook, ch 10. Work as for cuffs until band, when slightly stretched, fits front edge to neck. End off. Weave bands to front edges.

FINISHING: Do not block or press. Sew shoulder seams. Sew last row of sleeve to straight edge of armhole. Sew about 2″ at each side edge of sleeve to underarm edge of body,

then sew sleeve seams. Join cuff ends. Gather lower edge of sleeve to fit cuff and sew in place. Turn back front bands to right side and tack in place about ½″ in from edge of band.

Collar: With C hook from right side, beg after front band, work in sc around neck edge to front band. Ch 1, turn. Work 2 more rows in sc. Working in back lps as for cuff, work 1 row even. Continue to work in back lps, inc 1 st in every 10th st across. Work 1 row even. On next row, inc in every 12th st. Work 2 rows even. On next row inc in every 14th st. Work 2 rows even. End off. Fold collar in half to right side and tack in place about 1 inch from outer edge. From right side, working backwards from left to right on side edges and across lower edge of collar, work ch 1, hdc in first st, * ch 1, sk 1 sc, hdc in next st, repeat from * around, working through double thickness at side edges. End off. Work same edging on front bands and across top of bands through double thickness. Work edging around bottom of cuffs.

Sleeveless Cardigan

Note: Body is worked in one piece to underarm. With E (F) hook, ch 165 loosely.

Row 1 (right side): Dc in 4th ch from hook (turning ch counts as 1 dc), * sk 2 ch; in next ch work 5 dc for a shell, sk 3 ch, 5-dc shell in next ch, sk 2 ch; in next ch work dc, ch 1 and dc for a V st, repeat from * across, end sk 2 ch, 5-dc shell in next ch, sk 3 ch, 5-dc shell in next ch, sk 2 ch, dc in each of last 2 ch, 16 double shell pats. Ch 3, turn each row.

Row 2: Sk first dc (ch 3 counts as first dc), dc in next dc, * (work V st in 2nd dc of next shell. V st in 4th dc of same shell) twice, V st in ch-1 sp of next V st, repeat from * across, end (V st in 2nd dc of next shell, V st in 4th dc of same shell) twice, dc in each of last 2 dc.

Row 3: Sk first dc, dc in next dc, 5-dc shell in sp between next 2 V sts, 5-dc shell in sp between next 2 V sts, (these shells are above shells of row 1), * V st in next V st (shell in sp between next 2 V sts) twice, repeat from * across, end dc in each of last 2 dc. Piece should measure 32″ (36″) across. Repeat rows 2 and 3 for pat, until piece is 11″ from beg, end with row 2.

Divide for Back and Fronts

RIGHT FRONT: Work until there are 7 shells from front edge, dc in first dc of next V st. Ch 3, turn.

Shape Armhole and Neck

Row 1: Sk first dc, dc in 2nd dc of shell for armhole dec, V st in 4th dc of same shell, work to end. Ch 3, turn.

Row 2: Sk first dc, dc in next dc, 3 dc between next 2 V sts for a ½ shell (neck dec), work across row, end with ½ shell in last V st, dc in each of last 2 dc. Ch 3, turn each row.

Row 3: Sk first dc, dc in next dc, dc in center dc of ½ shell, work across row, end with dc in center dc of ½ shell, dc in each of last 2 dc.

Row 4: Sk first dc, dc in next dc, sk next dc, work across row, end with V st in last V st, sk next dc, dc in each of last 2 dc.

Row 5: Sk first dc, dc in next dc, work across row to last shell at front edge, work V st in 2nd dc of shell, dc in 4th dc of shell for neck dec, dc in each of last 2 dc.

Row 6: Sk first dc, dc in next dc, 3 dc for ½ shell in next V st, work pat to end.

Row 7: Work to last ½ shell, dc in center dc of ½ shell, dc in each of last 2 dc.

Row 8: Sk first dc, dc in next dc, sk next dc, work to end.

Row 9: Work to last V st, work dc in last V st, dc in each of last 2 dc.

Row 10: Sk first dc, dc in next dc, sk next dc, work to end.

Row 11: Work to last shell, V st in 2nd dc of shell, dc in 4th dc of same shell, dc in each of last 2 dc.

Row 12: Sk first dc, dc in next dc, ½ shell between next dc and V st, work to end.

Row 13: Work to ½ shell, dc in center dc of ½ shell, dc in each of last 2 dc.

Row 14: Sk first dc, dc in next dc, sk next dc, shell between next 2 V sts, work to end.

Row 15: Work to last shell, V st in 2nd dc of shell, dc in 4th dc of shell, dc in last 2 dc.

Row 16: Sk first dc, dc in next dc, sk 1 dc, dc in first dc of next V st, work to end.

Row 17: Work to last 3 dc, sk 1 dc, dc in each of last 2 dc.

If necessary, work in established pat until armhole measures 6¾″ (7¼″), end at armhole edge with a shell row. Ch 1, turn.

Shape Shoulder: Work sc in each of first 2 dc, sc in dc, ch 1 and next dc of V st, hdc in each dc of next 2 shell pats, dc in dc, ch 1 and dc of next V st, dc in each of last 2 dc. End off.

LEFT FRONT: Join yarn in the V st before the 7th shell from left front edge, ch 3 for first dc, work to front edge. Work to correspond to right front, reversing shaping.

BACK: Leaving 3 V sts with ½ V st at each side free for underarm, join yarn in 2nd dc of 4th V st, ch 3 for first dc, dc in next V st, shell between next 2 V sts, work across until there are 14 shell pats across back, dc in next V st, dc in first dc of next V st. Ch 3, turn each row.

Row 2: Sk first dc, dc in next dc, dc in 2nd dc of shell, V st in 4th dc of shell, work to last shell, V st in 2nd dc of shell, dc in 4th dc of shell, dc in last 2 sts.

Row 3: Sk first dc, dc in next dc, ½ shell between next dc and V st, work to last 2 V sts, V st in next V st, ½ shell between last V st and next dc, dc in last 2 sts.

Row 4: Sk first dc, dc in next dc, dc in center dc of ½ shell, work pat to last ½ shell, dc in center dc of ½ shell, dc in each of last 2 dc.

Row 5: Sk first dc, dc in next dc, sk next dc, work to last 3 dc, sk 1 dc, dc in each of last 2 dc.

Continue in established pat until armholes are same length as front armholes.

Shape shoulders same as on fronts. End off.

Waistband: With size C hook, ch 19. Work same as cuff of cardigan to 28″ (30″) or desired waist size. End off. Sew to lower edge of body easing in fullness.

FINISHING: Sew shoulder seams. Do not block or press.

Left Front Band: With size C hook, ch 9. Work same as waistband until band, when slightly stretched, fits front edge from lower edge to center back of neck. End off. Weave to left front edge and to center back of neck. Place markers on band for 5 buttons, having first one ½″ from lower edge and fifth one about ½″ below start of neck shaping.

Right Front Band: Work same as left front band forming buttonholes opposite markers as follows: Work 3 sts, ch 2, sk 2 sc, work to end.

On next row, work sc in each of 2 ch. Weave band to right front edge and to back of neck. Join band at center back. Work edging around front band and neck edges same as on cardigan.

Armholes: With size C hook, from right side, beg at underarm, work 1 row of sc around armholes, holding in to fit if necessary. Sl st in first sc. Ch 1, turn.

Rnds 2 and 3: Working in back lps only, sc in each sc. Join, ch 1, turn at end of rnd 2. Do not turn at end of rnd 3.

Rnd 4: Work edging same as on front neck. End off.

Openwork Crewneck Pullover

Alternating patterns of double crochet provide the fancy openwork texture of this classic and easy-to-make crewneck pullover.

SIZES: Directions are for small size (8–10). Changes for medium size (12–14) and large size (16–18) are in parentheses.

Body Bust Size: 31½″–32½″ (34″–36″; 38″–40″)

Blocked Bust Size: 36½″ (39½″–40½″)

MATERIALS: Nubby sport yarn, 17 (18–19) 1¾ oz. balls. Aluminum crochet hooks, sizes I and J (5½ and 6 mm).

GAUGE: 7 sts = 6″; 16 rows = 9″

Note: To dec 1 st, draw up a lp in each of 2 sts, yo and through all lps on hook.

SWEATER BACK

Lower Band: With I hook, ch 10.

Row 1: Hdc in 4th ch from hook (counts as 2 hdc), hdc in each ch—8 hdc. Ch 2, turn.

Row 2: Counting ch 2 as first hdc, * hdc around post of next hdc (yo, insert hook in sp before next st, bring hook across back of st and out in sp after st, draw up a lp and work off as a hdc), repeat from * across, end hdc in top of turning ch. Ch 2, turn. Repeat row 2 until band measures 14″ (15″–16″). Do not break off yarn.

Row 1: Work 52 (56–60) sc evenly spaced along side edge of band. Change to size J hook. Ch 3, turn.

Row 2: Counting ch 3 as first dc, dc in next st, * sk 1 st, dc in each of next 3 sts, long sc in skipped sc (passing hook in front of 3 dc, insert hook in skipped st and draw through a long lp to reach across 3 dc keeping yarn loose, work off as a sc), repeat from * across, end dc in each of last 2 sts. Ch 1, turn.

Row 3: Sc in each st across—52 (56–60) sts. Ch 3, turn.

Row 4: Repeat row 2.

Row 5: Repeat row 3.

Row 6: Counting ch 3 as first dc, dc in next st, * sk 1 st, dc in next st, dc back in skipped st, repeat from * across, end dc in each of last 2 sts. Ch 1, turn.

Row 7: Sc in each st across—52 (56–60) sts. Ch 3, turn. Repeat rows 2–7 for pat. Work until piece measures 14½″ from start, including border, or desired length to underarm, end row 2, 4, or 6. Piece should measure 18¼″ (19¾″–21¼″) wide.

Shape Armholes

Next Row: Sl st across 3 sts, work to last 3 sts. Dec 1 st 1 st in from each side of next 2 rows—42 (46–50) sts. Work until armholes measure 7¼″ (7¾″–8¼″) above bound-off sts, ending with a sc row. End off.

FRONT: Work same as back until armholes measure 5″ (5½″–6″) above bound-off sts, ending with a sc row—42 (46–50) sts.

Shape Neck

Next Row: Work 15 (16–17) sts. Working on this side only, dec 1 st at neck edge on next 2 sc rows—13 (14–15) sts. Work until armhole measures same as back to shoulder. End off. Return to last long row, sk center 12 (14–16) sts, join yarn and work other side to correspond, reversing shaping.

SLEEVES

Cuff: With 1 hook, ch 10. Work as for lower band on back until cuff measures 7″ (7½″–8″). Do not break off yarn. Change to size J hook.

Row 1: Work 36 (38–40) sc evenly spaced along side edge of cuff. Ch 3, turn.

Row 2: Counting ch 3 as first dc, dc in next st, * sk 1 st, dc in next st, dc back in skipped st (cross st made), repeat from * across, end dc in each of last 2 sts. Ch 3, turn.

Row 3: Counting ch 3 as first dc, dc in each of next 2 sts, * cross st over next 2 sts, repeat from * across, end dc in each of last 3 sts. Ch 3, turn. Repeat rows 2 and 3 for pat. Work until 17″ from start or desired length to underarm. Check gauge; piece should measure 12¾″ (13¼″–14″) wide.

Shape Cap

Next Row: Sl st across 3 sts, work to last 3 sts. Work in pat until cap measures 5″ (5½″–6″) above bound-off sts. Ch 1, turn.

Next Row: Sc in every other st across row. End off.

FINISHING: Weave shoulder, side, and sleeve seams, matching pat rows. From right side, with size I hook, work 1 row sc around neck edge, taking in slightly if necessary. Make sure opening goes over head easily.

Neckband: With size I hook, ch 6. Work as for lower band on back on 4 sts until band fits neck edge. End off. Weave band to neck edge, placing seam at center back. Weave back neckband seam. Do not block.

Banded Surplice Tunic

The colorful shell-stitch bands on this handsome tunic accentuate the design and give it eye-catching appeal as well. Worn with coordinated turtleneck and slacks, the tunic becomes the focal point of a beautifully dressy winter outfit.

SIZES: Directions for size 8. Changes for sizes 10, 12, 14, and 16 are in parentheses.

Body Bust Size: 31½″ (32½″–34″–36″–38″)

Blocked Bust Size: 32½″ (34½″–36½″–38″–39½″)

MATERIALS: Knitting worsted, 5 (5–5–6–6) 4-oz. skeins purple (A); 1 skein each of rose (B), green (C), and yellow (D). Crochet hook, size H.

GAUGE: 7 sts = 2″; 7 rows = 2″

PATTERN STITCH:

Row 1: Sc in 2nd ch from hook, * ch 1, sk 1 ch, sc in next ch, repeat from * across. Turn.

Row 2: Ch 1, sc in first sc, * ch 1, sk ch-1 sp, sc in next sc, repeat from * across. Turn. Repeat row 2 for pat always working ch 1 over ch-1 sp and sc over sc.

To bind off: At beg of a row, sl st loosely across specified sts; **at end of a row,** leave specified number of sts unworked.

To dec 1 st: At beg of a row, ch 1, pull up a lp in each of first 2 sts, yo and through 3 lps on hook; **at end of a row,** pull up a lp in each of last 2 sts, yo and through 3 lps on hook. **Next Row:** Work in pat as established (sc over each sc, ch 1 over a ch-1 sp).

TUNIC BACK: Beg at lower edge, with A, ch loosely 58 (62–66–68–70). Work in pat on 57 (61–65–67–69) sts for 21″. Piece should measure 16¼″ (17¼″–18½″–19″–19¾″) wide.

Shape Neck: Work in pat across 27 (29–31–31–33) sts, drop yarn, sk next 3 (3–3–5–3) sts, join another strand of A in next sc, ch 1, sc in same sc as joining, work in pat across—27 (29–31–31–33) sts each side. Keeping to pat as established, bind off 2 sts at each neck edge every row 10 times, then dec 1 st at same edge every row 2 (4–5–5–6) times—5 (5–6–6–7) sts each side. End off.

FRONT: Work same as for back for 18″—57 (61–65–67–69) sts.

Shape Neck: Work in pat across 27 (29–31–31–33) sts, drop yarn, sk next 3 (3–3–5–3) sts, join another strand of A in next st, ch 1, sc in same st as joining, work in pat as established across—27 (29–31–31–33) sts each side. Working on both sides at once, dec 1 st at each neck edge every row 22 (24–25–25–26) times—5 (5–6–6–7) sts each side. Work even until piece measures same as back. End off. Sew shoulder seams.

SLEEVES

Cuff: With B, ch 58 (58–62–62–66). Working in pat, work 1 row B, 1 row D, 1 row A—57 (57–61–61–65) sts. Mark last row for right side.

Row 4: With C, ch 1, sc in first sc, * shell of 3 dc in next D sc on row 2, sc in next A sc on row 3, repeat from * across—14 (14–15–15–16) shells. Do not turn.

Row 5: Join B at beg of last row, ch 1, sc in A sc in row 3, ch 1, * sc in center dc of 3-dc shell, ch 1, sc in A sc on row 3, ch 1, repeat from * across, end sc in last sc. Turn.

Row 6 (right side): With D, ch 2, 2 dc in first sc, * sc in next sc, shell of 3 dc in next sc, repeat from * across, end last repeat 2 dc in last sc. Turn.

Row 7 (wrong side): With A, ch 1, sc in first dc, ch 1, * sc in B sc on row 5, ch 1, sc in center dc of next 3-dc shell, ch 1, repeat from * across, end last repeat sc in last dc. End off.

From wrong side, join C in first ch on foundation ch, sc in first ch, * ch 1, sk next ch, sc in next ch, repeat from * across—57 (57–61–61–65) sts. With A, work in pat as for back until piece measures 16″ (16″–16½″–16½″–17″) from start. End off.

Right Front Band: Beg at center with B, ch 70. Work same as for sleeve cuff for 6 rows. Turn.

Next Row: With A, ch 1, sc in first dc, ch 1, * sc in B sc on row 5, sc in center dc of next 3-dc shell, ch 1, repeat from * across, end last repeat sc in last dc. End off.

From wrong side, join D in first ch on foundation ch, sc in first ch, * ch 1, sk next ch, sc in next ch, repeat from * across—69 sts.

Beg with row 3, work same as for sleeve cuff to end of row 7. Mark last row for lower edge of band. Pin lower edge of band to right neck edge, placing one narrow edge at right shoulder, other narrow edge 12" (12"–12"–12½"–12½") below left shoulder.

Left Front and Back Neckband: With B, ch 86. Work same as for sleeve cuff for 7 rows, having 21 shells on row 4. Mark last row for lower edge.

From wrong side, join D in first ch on foundation ch, * ch 1, sk next ch, sc in next ch, repeat from * across—85 sts.

Next Row: With A, ch 1, sc in first sc, ch 1, sc in next sc, * ch 1, pull up a lp in each of next 2 sc, yo hook and through 3 lps on hook, ch 1, sc in next sc, ch 1, sc in next sc, repeat from * 9 times, finish row—65 sts. Work sleeve cuff rows 4–7.

Pin lower edge of band around left front and back neck edge, placing one narrow edge at right shoulder, other narrow edge at front neck edge of right band as pictured. With center of sleeve at shoulder seam, sew sleeves to body. Sew side and sleeve seams. Steam lightly.

Infant's Sunny Stripe Outfit and Accessories

Make a baby's day brighter with any one of these sun-inspired projects: a suit, cap, booties, blanket, and cuddly turtle. The square-necked top buttons over both shoulders.

Sunshine Suit, Booties, and Hat

SIZES: Directions for 6 mos. Changes for 12 mos. are in parentheses.

Body Chest Size: 19″ (20″)

Blocked Chest Size: 20″ (21″)

MATERIALS: Sport yarn, 2 2-oz. skeins baby blue (A), 1 ball each medium blue (B), rose (C) and yellow (D) for sweater; 2 balls B and small amounts C and D for pants; small amounts A, B, C, and D for hat and booties. Crochet hooks, sizes E, G, H (3½, 4¼ and 5 mm). Six ⅜″ buttons.

GAUGE: 4 sc = 1″; 5 rows = 1″ (size H hook). 6 sc = 1″; 5 rows = 1″ (size E hook)

To Bind Off: At beg of row, sl st loosely across specified number of sts, ch 1, work in sc across; **at end of row,** leave specified number of sts unworked, ch 1, turn.

To Dec 1 Sc: Pull up a lp in each of 2 sc, yo and through 3 lps on hook.

To Inc 1 Sc: Work 2 sc in same sc.

SUIT

SWEATER FRONT: Beg at ribbing, with B and size G hook, ch 4.

Row 1: Sc in 2nd ch from hook and in each ch across—3 sc. Ch 1, turn each row.

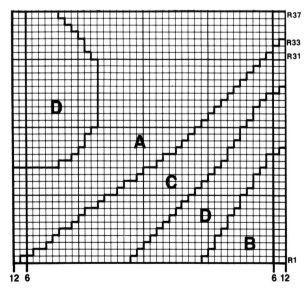

Row 2: Sc in back lp of each sc across. Repeat row 2 for ribbing until 38 (42) rows have been completed.

Next Row (wrong side): With B and size H hook, work 1 sc in each row of ribbing—38 (42) sc. Ch 1, turn each row. Working in sc, beg at lower right corner of chart, work until row 31 (33) of chart has been completed. Mark for armholes. Work even to top of chart, then with A, work until row 40 (42) has been completed. Check gauge; piece should measure 9½″ (10½″) wide.

Shape Neck: With A, work 10 (11) sc. Ch 1, turn. Continue in sc with A until 3¼″ (3½″) above armhole marker.

Buttonhole Row: With A, work 2 sc, ch 1, sk next sc, 4 (5) sc, ch 1, sk next sc, 2 sc. Ch 1, turn.

Next Row: Sc in each sc and ch-1 sp Ch 1, turn. Repeat last 2 rows once more for facing. End off.

Sk center 18 (20) sc on last long row. Join A and complete right shoulder same as left shoulder.

Neck Trim

Row 1: With B and size G hook, work sc in each row and st around neck edge, working 2 sc tog at each corner. Ch 1, turn each row.

Row 2: Work 1 sc in each sc, working 1 dec in each corner.

Row 3 (buttonhole row): Work 1 sc, ch 1, sk next sc, 1 sc in next sc, ch 1, sk next sc; working 1 dec in each corner, continue to work sc in each sc to last 4 sc, ch 1, sk next sc, 1 sc, ch 1, sk next sc, 1 sc. Ch 1, turn.

Row 4: Work sc in each sc and in each ch-1 sp, working 1 dec in each corner. End off.

BACK: Work to correspond to front, working from the lower left corner of chart. Leave a long strand of each color when ending off for sewing sweater tog. Omit buttonholes on shoulders.

SLEEVES: Beg at ribbing, with A and size G hook, ch 6 (8). Work in ribbing as for front until 21 (23) rows of 5 (7) sc have been completed. With A and size H hook, work 1 sc in each row of ribbing—21 (23) sc. Ch 1, turn each row. Work in sc, inc 3 sts on rows 2 and 6—27 (29) sc. Work even in sc until sleeve measures 6" (6½") from start. Piece should measure 6¾" (7¼") wide. End off.

FINISHING: Block to measurements. Sew side and sleeve seams. Fold 2 rows on front shoulders to inside so that buttonholes meet; hem in place, Buttonhole-st around buttonholes. Sew in sleeves. Sew buttons on shoulders opposite buttonholes. With D and size E hook, work 7 sunrays evenly spaced around sun consisting of 4 or 5 sc.

PANTS

First Leg: Beg at cuff ribbing, with B and size G hook, ch 9 (13).

Row 1: Sc in 2nd ch from hook and in each ch across—8 (12) sc. Ch 1, turn each row.

Row 2: Sc in back lp of each sc across. Repeat row 2 for ribbing until 24 (28) rows have been completed.

Next Row (wrong side): With size H hook and B, work 1 sc in each row of ribbing—24 (28) sc. Ch 1, turn each row.

Row 1: * Work 1 sc in each of next 3 sc, 2 sc in next sc, repeat from * across—30 (35) sc.

Row 2: * Work 2 sc in next st, 1 sc in each of next 4 sc, repeat from * across—36 (42) sc.

Row 3: Sc in each st. Change to D.

Row 4: Sc in each st.

Row 5: * Work 1 sc in each of next 5 sc, 2 sc in next sc, repeat from * across—42 (49) sc.

Row 6: Sc in each st. Change to C.

Rows 7–9: Sc in each st. Change to B.

Rows 10–29: Sc in each st.

Row 30: * Work 1 sc in each of next 5 sc, work 2 sc tog—dec made; repeat from * across—36 (42) sc. Piece should measure 9" (10½") wide. Work even in sc until piece is 8¼" (9") from start. End off.

Second Leg: Work same as first leg; do not end off. Ch 1, turn.

Next Row: Work across second leg, then continue across first leg; join with sl st to first sc; ch 1, turn each rnd. Continue in sc until piece measures 4½" (4¾") from crotch. End off.

Short Rows: Working with B on back 35 (39) sts only, work in sc for 2 rows. Work 1 rnd sc around entire waist. End off.

Waistband: With B and size G hook, ch 5. Work in ribbing as for cuff on 4 sc until piece is 16" (17") unstretched. End off.

FINISHING: Sew waistband to pants. With B and size G hook, make a ch 30" long. Sl st across ch. Lace through waistband. Sew leg seams.

BOOTIES
Beg at instep with A and size E hook, ch 6 (8).

Row 1: Sc in 2nd ch from hook and in each ch across—5 (7) sc. Ch 1, turn each row.

Row 2: Sc in back lp of each sc across. Repeat row 2 for 5 (7) rows more. Ch 23 (25), attach ch with sl st to first st of first row of instep, ch 1.

Rnd 1: Sc in same st as sl st, sc down side of instep, 2 sc in corner, 6 (8) sc across toe, 2 sc in corner, sc up side of instep, sc in each ch, sl st to first st.

Rnd 2: With C, sc in back lp of each sc; join. Repeat last rnd, working 1 rnd each D, B and A. End off.

Top: From right side, join A at center back, work 9 (10) sc, work 2 sts tog 5 times across instep, work 9 (10) sc; join each rnd, ch 1. Working in back lp of each sc, work 4 (6) more rnds.

Sole: Mark center of heel and toe.

Rnd 1: From wrong side, with B and size E hook, beg at heel, work 1 sc, dec 1 st, work to toe, dec 1 st, work to heel, dec 1 st, join.

Rnd 2: Dec 1 sc, sc to 2 sts before toe marker, dec 1 st, sc in center of toe, dec 1 st, sc to last 2 sts, dec 1 st. End off.

FINISHING: Weave sole seam. With B and

hook size E, make a ch about 11″ long; weave through cuff.

HAT
Beg at face edge, with C and size H hook, ch 44 (46).

Row 1: Sc in 2nd ch from hook and in each ch across—43 (45) sc. Ch 1, turn each row.

Row 2: Sc in each st across.

Rows 3 and 4: With D, work in sc.

Rows 5 and 6: With B, work in sc.

Row 7 (right side): With A, sc in back lp of each sc across. Work even in sc until hat measures 4″ (4½″) from start. Work in sc, dec 1 st each side of next 6 rows—31 (33) sc. End off.

FINISHING: From right side, with B and size H hook, work 1 row sc along neck and back edge of hat. Sew back seam.

Ties: With B and size H hook, ch 38. Sl st in each ch across; sc across front of hat, ch 39 for other tie. Sl st in ch across. End off.

Pompom: With D, make a 2″ pompom and sew to top of hat.

Turtle

MATERIALS: Sport yarn, 1 2-oz. skein baby blue (A), 1 oz. each medium blue (B), rose (C) and yellow (D). Crochet hook, size E. Polyester fiberfill for stuffing.

GAUGE: 6 sc = 1″; 5 rows = 1″

Note: Work tightly.

SHELL: With B, ch 2.

Rnd 1: 6 sc in 2nd ch from hook.

Rnd 2: 2 sc in each sc around.

Rnd 3: * Sc in next sc, 2 sc in next sc, repeat from * around—18 sc.

Rnd 4: * Sc in 2 sc, 2 sc in next sc, repeat from * around—24 sc.

Rnd 5: * Sc in 3 sc, 2 sc in next sc, repeat from * around—30 sc.

Rnd 6: * Sc in next sc, 2 sc in next sc, sc in each of next 4 sc, repeat from * around—35 sc.

Rnd 7: Sc in 4 sc, * 2 sc in next sc, sc in 5 sc, repeat from * around, end sc in last sc—40 sc. Change to D.

Rnd 8: Working in back lp of sc only, * work 2 sc in next sc, sc in next 7 sc, repeat from * around—45 sc.

Rnd 9: Working in back lps, sc in 5 sc, * 2 sc in next sc, sc in 4 sc, repeat from * around—53 sc.

Rnd 10: Working in back lps, sc in 5 sc, * 2 sc in next sc, sc in 5 sc, repeat from * around—61 sc.

Rnd 11: Sc in 5 sc, * 2 sc in next sc, sc in 6 sc, repeat from * around—69 sc. Change to C. Work 8 rnds even in sc. End off. Fold 2 rnds to inside and hem in place.

Feet (make 4): With A, ch 4; join with sl st to form ring.

Next Rnd: Work 7 sc in ring. Work even in sc unil piece measures 1½″, join with sl st. End off. At beg of foot, with A, sc in 3 sts. Work 4 rows sc. End off, leaving 4″ strand of yarn. Draw yarn through the 3 sts. Fold 2 sc rows to inside, stitch bottom of foot closed.

Head: With A, ch 3, join with sl st to form ring. Ch 1.

Next Rnd: Work 11 sc in ring. Work 4 rnds of 11 sc.

Next Rnd: 2 sc in each of next 3 sc, sc in each of next 2 sc, (work next 2 sc tog) 3 times, sc in next sc.

Next Rnd: Sc in next sc, 2 sc in next 3 sts, sc in next sc, dec 3 sc.

Next Rnd: Repeat last rnd. End off. With C, work French knots for eyes on each side of head.

Tail: With A, ch 2; 3 sc in 2nd ch from hook. Work 3 rnds sc. Pull yarn through all 3 sts. End off.

Bottom: With A, work same as shell to last 8 rows. End off.

FINISHING: Stuff head and legs. Do not stuff tail. Pin extended part of head, legs, and tail in place under shell. Sew in place. Add bottom of shell, folding under 1 row. Sew in place inside shell, leaving small opening. Stuff. Close opening. Sew upper part of head to front of shell.

Blanket

SIZE: 32″ × 32″.

MATERIALS: Sport yarn, 3 2-oz. skeins baby blue (A), 2 balls rose (C), and 1 ball each medium blue (B) and yellow (D). Crochet hook, size H.

GAUGE: 4 sts = 1″; 4 rows = 1″

PATTERN: 5 rows A, 1 row D, 2 rows C, 1 row B, 2 rows C, 1 row D.
   Beg at corner, with B, ch 2.

Row 1: Sc in 2nd ch from hook. Ch 1, turn each row.

Row 2: Work 3 sc in sc.

Row 3: Work 2 sc in first sc, sc in next sc, 2 sc in last sc. Change to C. Work 2 rows sc, inc 1 st at each side of each row. Change to D.

Next Row: Work 1 row sc, inc 1 st at each side. Following stripe pat, work until 6 sets of stripe pat are completed, inc 1 st each side of every row. Work another set of stripe pat until Color B row has been completed. Complete this pat stripe and work 6 more sets of stripe pat, dec 1 st each side of every row. Work 5 rows A, 1 row D, 2 rows C, 3 rows B, dec 1 st each side of every row. End off.

Border

Row 1: From right side, with B, work 1 row dc around entire blanket, working 3 dc in each corner, sl st to first st. Ch 2, turn.

Row 2: Work 1 row dc working 3 dc in each corner. End off.

FINISHING: Block to size and shape.

A Party Pinafore and Blouse with Dual Roles

An airy, picot-edged, white pinafore of lacy knot stitches provides a cool cover-up for a hot summer's day. It also makes a lovely complement to a party dress of any color, and, in that guise, will last for more than one season. The flowery filet-crocheted blouse doubles as a cardigan because its buttoned back can be worn equally well to the front.

Party Blouse

SIZES: Directions for small size (2–4). Changes for medium size (6–8) are in parentheses.

Body Chest Size: 21″–23″ (24″–27″)

Blocked Chest Size (closed): 23″ (27″)

MATERIALS: Baby yarn, 2 2-oz. skeins. Steel crochet hook, No. 1. Aluminum crochet hook, size D (E). Five ½″ buttons.

GAUGE: 7 sts = 1″; 3 rows = 1″ (No. 1 hook). Each motif = 2⅞″ (3¼″) square.

Note: Crochet hook size and gauge determine size of motifs.

BLOUSE FRONT: Beg at lower edge, with No. 1 hook, ch 86 (94).

Row 1 (right side): Dc in 6th ch from hook (counts as dc, ch 1, dc), * ch 1, sk next ch, dc in next ch, repeat from * across—42 (46) dc. Turn.

Row 2: Ch 4, sk first ch-1 sp, dc in next dc, * ch 1, dc in next dc, repeat from * across, end ch 1, dc in 3rd ch of turning ch. Turn. Repeat last row until piece measures 8″ (9″) from start. Check gauge; piece should measure 12″ (13″) wide. End off.

BACK (make 2): Beg at lower edge, with No. 1 hook, ch 44 (48). Work same as for front on 21 (23) dc until piece measures same as front. Check gauge; piece should measure 6″ (6½″) wide. End off.

MOTIFS (make 16): Beg at center with size D (E) hook, ch 6, sl st in first ch to form ring.

Rnd 1: Ch 5, (dc in ring, ch 2) 7 times, sl st in 3rd ch of ch 5—8 ch-2 sps.

Rnd 2: In each sp around work sc, hdc, dc, hdc, sc—8 petals.

Rnd 3: (Working behind petals, sc around post of next dc of rnd 1, ch 7) 8 times, sl st in first sc—8 sps.

Rnd 4: In each sp around work sc, hdc, 3 dc, hdc, sc—8 petals.

Rnd 5: Sl st in each st to center dc of petal, * ch 5, tr in sp between sc of last petal and next petal (corner), ch 5, sc in center dc of next petal, ch 7, sc in center dc of next petal, repeat from * around, end ch 5, sc in sl st at center of first petal. End off.

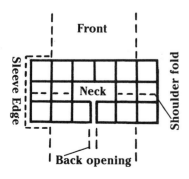

FINISHING: Following chart, sew motifs tog through scs and trs on last rnd, having trs meeting at corners. Sew front to 4 center motifs on front of yoke. Sew each back to 2 center motifs on back of yoke. Sew side seams. Sew front and back of sleeve edge motifs tog at underarm.

Right Back Center Band: Join yarn in tr at upper right back neck edge.

Row 1: With No. 1 hook, ch 1, sc in same st, sc across right back edge, being careful to keep work flat, end lower edge. Ch 1, turn each row.

Rows 2 and 3: Sc in each sc across. End off.

Left Back Center Band: Join yarn in tr at lower left back edge.

Row 1: With No. 1 hook, ch 1, work same number of sc across left back edge as on right back edge. Ch 1, turn each row.

With pins, mark position of 5 buttonholes evenly spaced on left center edge, first pin ½″ above lower edge, 5th pin ½″ below neck edge.

Row 2: * Sc in each sc to within 1 sc of pin, ch 2, sk next 2 sc, sc in next sc, repeat from * 4 times, sc in each remaining sc.

Row 3: Sc in each sc and ch across, end neck edge. Do not turn.

Next Row (picot row): * Ch 3, sl st in 3rd ch from hook (picot made), sc in next 6 sts, sk next st, repeat from * around neck edge. End off.

Lower Edging: From right side, join yarn in lower right back center edge, work picot edging around lower edge same as for neck, end lower left back center edge. End off.

Work same picot edging around lower edge of each sleeve.

Steam press lightly; do not flatten motif petals. Sew on buttons.

Party Pinafore

SIZES: Directions for size 2. Changes for sizes 4, 6, and 8 are in parentheses.

Body Chest Size: 21″ (23″–24″–27″).

MATERIALS: Sport yarn, 4 (6–7–8) 1-oz. balls. Steel crochet hook, No. 2. Two buttons. Two hooks and eyes.

GAUGE: 9 pats = 4″; 3 rows = 1″; 4 sc = 1″

PATTERN

Row 1: Hdc in 3rd ch from hook, * draw up a ½″ lp on hook, yo and through long lp; insert hook between long lp and single strand at back of long lp, yo hook, draw lp through, yo hook and through 2 lps on hook (knot-st made), sk next 2 ch, hdc in next ch (pat made), repeat from * across. Ch 2, turn.

Row 2: Sk first hdc, * make knot-st, hdc in next hdc, repeat from * across, end hdc in top of ch 2. Ch 2, turn. Repeat row 2 for pat.

SKIRT: Beg at lower edge above ruffle, ch 288 (300–312–324). Work in pat on 95 (99–103–107) pats for 2″. Check gauge; piece should measure 42″ (44″–46″–47½″) wide.

Next Row (dec row): Work 22 (23–24–25) pats, work knot-st, yo hook, pull up a lp in each of next 2 hdc, yo hook and through 4 lps on hook (1 pat dec), work next 47 (49–51–53) pats, work 1 pat dec as before, finish row. Work even in pat for 2″.

Next Row (dec row): Work 21 (22–23–24) pats, dec 1 pat, work next 47 (49–51–53) pats, dec 1 pat, finish row. Work even in pat for 2″. Repeat dec row every 2″ twice more, working 1 less pat before and after decs—87 (91–95–99) pats. Work even if necessary until piece is 8″ (9½″–10″–11″) from start or 2″ less than desired skirt length. Ch 1, turn.

Waistband

Row 1: Sc in each knot-st across—87 (91–95–99) sc. Ch 1, turn each row.

Rows 2–5: Sc in each sc. End off.

Bib: Sk 30 (31–32–33) sc, join yarn in next sc, ch 2; skipping 1 sc between pats, work 13 (14–15–16) pats. Ch 2, turn. Work even until bib measures 4″ (4″–4½″–5″) from start. Ch 2, turn.

Straps: Work 3 (3–3–4) pats. Ch 2, turn. Work even until strap is 15″ (16″–17″–18″) from start. End off. Join yarn in 3rd (3rd–3rd–4th) pat from end of bib, work 2nd strap the same.

Strap Ruffles: Join yarn in side edge of strap 7½″ (8″–8½″–9″) above waistband. Working in edge of strap, work a pat in edge of next 14 (15–16–17) rows. Ch 1, turn.

Next Row: Sl st in first hdc, sl st in knot, sl st in lp of same knot-st pat, sl st in next hdc, ch 2, work in pat to within last pat. Ch 1, turn. Repeat last row once. Ch 3, turn.

Next Row: Hdc in hdc, * ch 3, hdc in next hdc, repeat from * across. End off. Work same ruffle on edge of other strap.

Skirt Ruffle

Row 1: Join yarn in first ch of starting ch at lower edge of skirt. Ch 2, hdc in same ch, * work knot-st, sk next 2 ch, hdc in next ch, (work knot-st, sk 1 ch, hdc in next ch) 3 times, repeat from * around. Ch 2, turn. Work even in pat for 2 more rows. End off.

FINISHING: Block pinafore. Weave back seam, leaving upper 3″ open.

Edging: Join yarn at start of bib, * work hdc, dc in edge of next row, ch 3, sl st in 3rd ch from hook (picot made), dc, hdc in edge of next row, repeat from * around straps, neck and bib, end at waistline. End off.

Edging for Skirt Ruffle: Work (hdc, dc, picot, dc, hdc) in each pat around lower edge.

Try on pinafore, and pin for placement of waist hooks and eyes and position of crossed straps. Sew buttons at waistline for straps. Use spaces between pats on straps for buttonholes.

PART IV
CROCHETED ACCESSORIES AND TOYS

As might be expected in an assortment of crochet accessories, this one includes a hat, scarf, and mittens, as well as some lovely lacy stoles. It also comprises a smart set of colorful totes of different shapes in addition to matching rugs and pillows in beautiful designs that combine crochet and cross-stitch. The dolls are all from Mother Goose.

Filagree Summer Shawls

One of the most useful accessories to have for summer wear is an elegant shawl to chase away any chill without adding too much warmth. Both of these shawls answer that need, while providing a choice of equally beautiful designs, a spiderweb or a fan.

Fan-Patterned Shawl

SIZE: 56″ wide; 33″ deep at center back, plus fringe.

MATERIALS: Mercerized knitting and crochet cotton, about 1400 yards. Steel crochet hook, No. 1.

GAUGE: 3 meshes (ch 2, dc) = 1″

SHAWL: Beg at lower center back, ch 19.

Row 1: Dc in 7th ch from hook, (ch 2, sk next 2 ch, dc in next ch) 4 times. Ch 5, turn each row.

Row 2: (Dc, ch 2, dc) in first ch-2 sp, (ch 2, dc in next ch-2 sp) 3 times, ch 2, (dc, ch 2, dc) in last sp—7 dc.

Row 3: (Dc, ch 2, dc) in first ch-2 sp, * ch 2, dc in next ch-2 sp, repeat from * across, end ch 2, (dc, ch 2, dc) in last ch-2 sp (do not work in turning ch)—8 dc.

Rows 4–9: Repeat row 3—14 dc.

Row 10: * (Dc, ch 2, dc) in first ch-2 sp, (ch 2, dc in next ch-2 sp) 5 times, ch 2, * 5 dc in next ch-2 sp, ch 2, # (dc in next ch-2 sp, ch 2) 5 times, (dc, ch 2, dc) in last ch-2 sp #.

Row 11: Work from first * to 2nd * on row 10, dc in next ch-2 sp, dc in each of next 5 dc, dc in next ch-2 sp, ch 2, work from first # to 2nd # on row 10.

Row 12: Work from first * to 2nd * on row 10, dc in next ch-2 sp, dc in each of next 7 dc, dc in next ch-2 sp, ch 2, work from first # to 2nd # on row 10.

Row 13: Work from first * to 2nd * on row 10, 5 dc in next sp, ch 4, sk next 3 dc, sc in next dc, ch 4, sk next dc, sc in next dc, ch 4, 5 dc in next sp, ch 2, work from first # to 2nd # on row 10.

Row 14: Work from first * to 2nd * on row 10, dc in next sp, dc in each of next 5 dc, dc in next sp, ch 4, sc in next sp, ch 4, dc in next sp, dc in each of next 5 dc, dc in next sp, ch 2, work from first # to 2nd # on row 10.

Row 15: Work from first * to 2nd * on row 10, (dc in next sp, dc in each of next 7 dc, dc in next sp, ch 2) twice, work from first # to 2nd # on row 10.

Row 16: Work from first * to 2nd * on row 10, (5 dc in next sp, ch 4, sk next 3 dc, sc in next dc, ch 4, sk next dc, sc in next dc, ch 4) twice, 5 dc in next sp, ch 2, work from first # to 2nd # on row 10.

Row 17: Work from first * to 2nd * on row 10, (dc in next sp, dc in each of next 5 dc, dc in next sp, ch 4, sc in next sp, ch 4) twice, dc in next sp, dc in each of next 5 dc, dc in next sp, ch 2, work from first # to 2nd # on row 10.

Row 18: Work from first * to 2nd * on row 10, (dc in next sp, dc in each of next 7 dc, dc in next sp, ch 2) 3 times, work from first # to 2nd # on row 10—3 pats.

Rows 19–99: Repeat rows 16–18 having 1 more pat every 3 rows. Ch 1, turn at end of last row.

Row 100: Sc in each st across. End off.

FINISHING: Steam lightly.

FRINGE: Wind yarn around 8″-wide piece of cardboard. Cut one end. With 8 strands tog, fold strands in half, pull loop end through ch-5 turning ch, pull ends through loop; tighten knot. Knot a fringe in each turning ch on sides of shawl. Trim ends evenly.

Spiderweb Shawl

SIZE: 56″ wide; 28″ deep at center back, plus fringe.

MATERIALS: Mercerized knitting and crochet cotton, about 1200 yards. Steel crochet hook, No. 1.

GAUGE: 3 meshes (ch 2, dc) = 1″

SHAWL: Beg at lower center back, ch 10; join with a sl st to form ring.

Row 1: Ch 5, dc in ring, (ch 2, dc in ring) 9 times. Ch 5, turn each row.

Row 2: (Dc, ch 2, dc) in first ch-2 sp, * (ch 2, dc in next ch-2 sp) 3 times, (ch 2, dc) twice in next ch-2 sp, repeat from * once—12 dc, plus turning ch.

Row 3: (Dc, ch 2, dc) in first ch-2 sp, ch 2, dc in next ch-2 sp, (ch 2, dc) twice in next ch-2 sp, ch 2, dc in next ch-2 sp, ch 2, 3 dc in next ch-2 sp, ch 3, dc in next ch-2 sp, ch 3, 3 dc in next ch-2 sp, ch 2, dc in next ch-2 sp, (ch 2, dc) twice in next ch-2 sp, ch 2, dc in next ch-2 sp, (ch 2, dc) twice in next ch-2 sp.

Row 4: * (Dc, ch 2, dc) in first ch-2 sp, (ch 2, dc in next ch-2 sp) 4 times, ch 2, 2 dc in next ch-2 sp, dc in dc * ch 3, sc in next ch-2 sp, sc in dc, sc in next ch-2 sp, ch 3, sk next 2 dc, # dc in next dc, 2 dc in ch-2 sp, (ch 2, dc in next ch-2 sp) 4 times, (ch 2, dc) twice in next ch-2 sp #.

Row 5: Work from first * to 2nd * on row 4, ch 3, sc in next ch-3 sp, sc in each of next 3 sc, sc in next ch-3 sp, ch 3, sk next 2 dc, work from first # to 2nd # on row 4.

Row 6: Work from first * to 2nd * on row 4, ch 2, sk next dc, dc in next dc, 2 dc in next sp, ch 3, sk next sc, sc in each of next 3 sc, ch 3, 2 dc in next sp, dc in next dc, ch 2, sk next dc, work from first # to 2nd # on row 4.

Row 7: Work from first * to 2nd * on row 4, ch 3, dc in next ch-2 sp, ch 3, sk next 2 dc, dc in next dc, 2 dc in next ch-3 sp, ch 3, sk next sc, dc in next sc, ch 3, 2 dc in next ch-3 sp, dc in next dc, ch 3, dc in next ch-2 sp, ch 2, sk next 2 dc, work from first # to 2nd # on row 4.

Row 8: Work from first * to 2nd * on row 4, ch 3, sc in next sp, sc in dc, sc in next sp, ch 3, sk next 2 dc, dc in next dc, 2 dc in next sp, ch 2, 2 dc in next sp, dc in first dc, ch 3, sc in next sp, sc in dc, sc in next sp, ch 3, sk next 2 dc, work from first # to 2nd # on row 4.

Row 9: Work from first * to 2nd * on row 4, ch 3, sc in next sp, sc in each of next 3 sc, sc in next sp, ch 3, sk next 2 dc, dc in next dc, dc in sp, dc in next dc, ch 3, sc in next sp, sc in each of next 3 sc, sc in next sp, ch 3, sk next 2 dc, work from first # to 2nd # on row 4.

Row 10: Work from first * to 2nd * on row 4, (ch 3, sk next dc, dc, in next dc, 2 dc in sp, ch 3, sk next sc, sc in each of next 3 sc, ch 3, 2 dc in next sp, dc in first dc) twice, ch 2, sk next dc, work from first # to 2nd # on row 4.

Row 11: Work from first * to 2nd * on row 4, (ch 3, dc in next sp, ch 3, sk next 2 dc, dc in next dc, 2 dc in sp, ch 3, sk next sc, dc in next sc, ch 3, 2 dc in next sp, dc in next dc) twice, ch 3, dc in next sp, ch 3, sk next 2 dc, work from first # to 2nd # on row 4.

Row 12: Work from first * to 2nd * on row 4, (ch 3, sc in next sp, sc in next dc, sc in next sp, ch 3, sk next 2 dc, dc in next dc, 2 dc in next sp, ch 2, 2 dc in next sp, dc in next dc) twice, ch 3, sc in next sp, sc in next dc, sc in next sp, ch 3, sk next 2 dc, work from first # to 2nd # on row 4.

Row 13: Work from first * to 2nd * on row 4, (ch 3, sc in next sp, sc in each of next 3 sc, sc in next sp, ch 3, sk next 2 dc, dc in next dc, dc in next sp, dc in next dc) twice, ch 3, sc in next sp, sc in each of next 3 sc, sc in next sp, ch 3, sk next 2 dc, work from first # to 2nd # on row 4.

Row 14: Work from first * to 2nd * on row 4, (ch 2, sk next dc, dc in next dc, 2 dc in next sp, ch 3, sk next sc, sc in each of next 3 sc, ch 3, 2 dc in next sp, dc in next dc) 3 times, ch 2, sk next dc, work from first # to 2nd # on row 4.

Row 15: Work from first * to 2nd * on row 4, (ch 3, dc in next sp, ch 3, sk next 2 dc, dc in next dc, 2 dc in sp, ch 3, sk next sc, dc in next sc, ch 3, 2 dc in next sp, dc in next dc) 3 times, ch 3, dc in next sp, ch 3, sk next 2 dc, work from first # to 2nd # on row 4—3 pats.

Rows 16–101: Repeat rows 12–15 having 1 more pat every 4 rows—25 pats. Ch 1, turn at end of last row.

Row 102: Sc in each st across. End off.

FINISHING: Steam lightly.

FRINGE: Wind yarn around 9″-wide piece of cardboard. Cut one end. With 7 strands tog, fold strands in half, pull loop end through ch-5 turning ch, pull ends through loop; tighten knot. Knot a fringe in each turning ch on sides of shawl. Trim ends evenly.

Chill-chasing Hat, Scarf, and Mittens

For an indispensable, easy-to-make accessory that makes a perfect gift too, try one or all of the items in this trio. All three are worked in single crochet, and the versatile hat, which can be worn three ways (as shown), can be completed in a single evening.

SIZES: Hat, medium. Mittens, 6–7. Scarf, 6″ × 60″.

MATERIALS: Knitting worsted, 9 2-oz. balls of desired color. (Pictured colors are bright red, navy blue, gold, green, and brick red.) Crochet hook, size J.

GAUGE: 7 sc = 2″ (single strand of yarn); 5 sc = 2″ (double strand of yarn).

Hat

Beg at top of crown, with one strand of yarn, ch 2.

Rnd 1: 6 sc in 2nd ch from hook.

Rnd 2: 2 sc in each sc around.

Rnd 3: (Sc in next sc, 2 sc in next sc) 6 times—18 sc.

Rnd 4: (2 sc in next sc, sc in each of next 2 sc) 6 times—24 sc.

Rnd 5: (Sc in each of next 3 sc, 2 sc in next sc) 6 times—30 sc.

Rnd 6: (Sc in each of next 2 sc, 2 sc in next sc) 10 times—40 sc.

Rnd 7: (Sc in each of next 3 sc, 2 sc in next sc) 10 times—50 sc.

Rnd 8: (Sc in each of next 4 sc, 2 sc in next sc) 10 times—60 sc. Mark end of last rnd. Work even on 60 sc for 13 rnds. End off.

Brim: With double strand of yarn, ch 22.

Row 1: Sc in 2nd ch from hook and in each ch—21 sc. Ch 1, turn each row.

Row 2: Sc in back lp of each sc. Repeat row 2 until there are 30 ridges (60 rows). End off. Sew last row to starting ch. With seam at back of hat, sew one edge of brim to last rnd of hat.

Mittens

Beg at top of mitten, with one strand of yarn, ch 2.

Rnd 1: 6 sc in 2nd ch from hook.

Rnd 2: 2 sc in each sc around.

Rnd 3: (Sc in next sc, 2 sc in next sc) 6 times—18 sc.

Rnd 4: (Sc in each of next 2 sc, 2 sc in next sc) 6 times—24 sc.

Rnds 5–19: Work even on 24 sc for 15 rnds.

Rnd 20 (thumb opening): Ch 4, sk 4 sc, sc in next sc and each sc around.

Rnd 21: Sc in each of 4 ch, sc in each sc around.

Rnds 22–28: Work even on 24 sc for 7 rnds. End off.

Thumb: Join yarn at beg of thumb opening, sc in each of 4 skipped sc, sc in st at side of thumb, sc in each of 4 ch sts, sc in st at side of thumb—10 sc. Work even on 10 sc for 7 rnds.

Next Rnd: (Draw up a lp in each of next 2 sts, yo and through 3 lps on hook) 5 times. Cut yarn, leaving 8″ end. Thread end in yarn needle and draw through last 5 sts. Pull sts tog tightly; fasten securely. Press mitten flat with thumb at outer edge of palm.

Cuff: With double strand of yarn, ch 11. Work as for brim of hat on 10 sc for 12 ridges (24 rows). Sew last row to starting ch. Sew one edge of cuff to last rnd of mitten, seam at center of palm.

Make 2nd mitten the same, pressing mitten with thumb at opposite side of palm.

String for Mittens: With double strand of yarn, ch 140. Sl st in each ch. Sew an end to each mitten at inner side edge of palm just above cuff.

Scarf

With double strand of yarn, make a ch about 60″ long.

Row 1: Sc in 2nd ch from hook and in each ch across. Ch 1, turn each row.

Row 2: Sc in back lp of each sc. Repeat row 2 until there are 9 ridges (18 rows). End off.

Folk Art Pillows and Rugs

Highly decorative pillows and rugs in intriguing folk art patterns are easy to create by embroidering single crochet with cross-stitches in brightly-colored rug yarns. Either of these designs would be suitable for a traditional or modern country environment, and, of course, the colors can be changed to suit any room.

SIZES: Cushions, 24″ square. Rugs, 24″ × 34″.

MATERIALS: Craft & rug yarn, 10 4-oz. skeins of yellow for one pillow and rug set. For set with large flower design, 2 skeins each of deep rose and red, 1 skein each of blue, green, and brown. For set with small flower design, 1 skein each of deep rose, red, green,

brown and dark turquoise. Crochet hook, size K. Rug needles. For each pillow, ¾ yard 60″-wide fabric. Two 1 lb. bags of polyester fiberfill.

GAUGE: 2 sc = 1″; 2 rows = 1″ (double strand).

Large Flower Cushion

With double strand of yellow, ch 50

Row 1: Sc in 2nd ch from hook and in each ch across—49 sc. Ch 1, turn each row.

Row 2: Sc in each sc across. Repeat row 2 until there are 52 rows. Work 1 rnd sc around entire pillow top, working 3 sc in each corner. Join; end off.

Following chart and using yarn double in rug needle, embroider design in cross-stitch, working 1 cross-stitch over 1 sc. Row 1 of chart is row 1 of crochet.

Make pillow same size as cushion top; sew cushion top to pillow with matching sewing thread.

Large Flower Rug

Work as for cushion until there are 73 rows. Work 1 row sc on each lengthwise edge of rug.

Following chart and using yarn double in rug needle, embroider design in cross-stitch, working 1 cross-stitch over 1 sc. Work to B on chart; then repeat from A to top of chart.

Small Flower Cushion

With double strand of yellow, ch 50.

Row 1: Sc in 2nd ch from hook and in each ch across—49 sc. Ch 1, turn each row.

Row 2: Sc in each sc across. Repeat row 2 until there are 49 rows. Work 1 rnd sc around entire pillow top, working 3 sc in each corner. Join; end off.

Following chart and using yarn double in rug needle, embroider design in cross-stitch, working 1 cross-stitch over 1 sc. Row 1 of chart is row 1 of crochet.

Make pillow same size as cushion top; sew cushion top to pillow using matching sewing thread.

⊡ **Red**	◪ **Blue**
▨ **Brown**	☑ **Green**
⊟ **Deep Rose**	⊞ **Turquoise**

Small Flower Rug

Work as for cushion until there are 70 rows. Following chart and using yarn double in rug needle, embroider design in cross-stitch, working 1 cross-stitch over 1 sc. On center flower design, leave 2 rows free before, after, and between flowers instead of 1 row as on cushion, but work border design as shown. Work to B on chart, then repeat from A to top of chart. If desired, work 1 rnd sc around entire rug, working 3 sc in each corner. Join; end off.

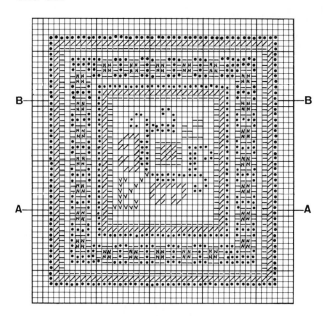

Large Flower Chart

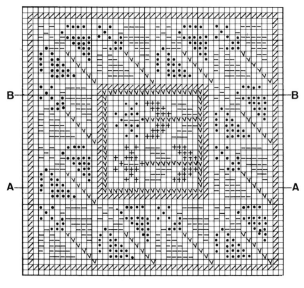

Small Flower Chart

Totes of All Persuasions

Whether you are heading for the beach or just planning a quick outing in another direction, you are sure to find one of these colorful totes a welcome companion. They are varied in both shape and pattern to suit a variety of needs and tastes, and all are worked in easy stitches.

Tapered Tote

SIZE: 16″ long.

MATERIALS: Rug yarn, 3 60-yd. skeins each of hemlock (A), brick (B), and gold (C). Crochet hook, size J (6 mm).

GAUGE: 3 sts = 1″; 3 rows dc = 2″

TOTE: Beg at bottom, with C, ch 25.

Rnd 1: 3 sc in 2nd ch from hook, sc in next 22 ch, 3 sc in last ch; working back on opposite side of ch, sc in next 22 ch.

Rnd 2: (2 sc in each of 3 sc at end, sc in 22 sc) twice.

Rnd 3: Sc in each sc around—56 sc.

Rnd 4: Work in sc, inc 6 sc at each end.

Rnd 5: Sc in each sc around—68 sc.

Rnd 6: Work in sc, inc 7 sc at each end.

Rnd 7: Sc in each sc around—82 sc.

Rnd 8: Ch 2 (counts as first dc), dc in back lp of next sc and in back lp of each sc around. Join to top of ch 2. End off.

Rnd 9: Join A in any dc at one end of bag; ch 2, dc in each dc around, join to top of ch 2. End off.

Rnd 10: With B, repeat rnd 9.

Rnd 11: With C, repeat rnd 9. Working 1 rnd each of A, B, and C, repeat rnd 9 until 3rd A rnd has been completed.

Next Rnd: Join B; ch 2, * dc in 7 dc, (yo hook, pull up a lp in next dc, yo and through 2 lps) twice (a dec made), repeat from * around, join. End off. Work even in stripe pattern on 73 dc for 3 rnds.

Next Rnd: Join C; ch 2, * dc in 6 dc, dec 1 dc over next 2 sts, repeat from * around, join. End off. Work even in stripe pattern on 64 dc for 3 rnds.

Next Rnd: Join A; ch 2, * dc in 5 dc, dec 1 dc over next 2 sts, repeat from * around, join. End off. Work even in stripe pattern on 55 dc for 6 rnds.

Picot Edging: With A, * sc in next 4 dc, ch 3, sc in 3rd ch from hook for picot, repeat from * around. End off.

Drawstrings (make 2): With A, B, and C held tog, ch 75. End off. Beg at one side of bag, weave a drawstring through last dc rnd, weaving under and over 3 dc. Sew ends tog securely. Repeat from other side of bag with 2nd drawstring.

Circular Tote

SIZE: 10″ high.

MATERIALS: Rug yarn, 3 60-yd. skeins of gold (G), 1 skein each of orange (O), brick (B), and hemlock (H). Crochet hook, size J (6 mm).

GAUGE: 3 sts = 1″; 2 rnds = 1″

TOTE: Beg at bottom, with G, ch 2.

Rnd 1: 5 hdc in first ch.

Rnd 2: 2 hdc in each hdc around.

Rnd 3: 2 hdc in each hdc around—20 hdc.

Rnd 4: (Hdc in next hdc, 2 hdc in next hdc) 10 times.

Rnd 5: (Hdc in each of 2 hdc, 2 hdc in next hdc) 10 times—40 hdc.

Rnd 6: (Hdc in each of 3 hdc, 2 hdc in next hdc) 10 times—50 hdc.

Rnd 7: (Hdc in each of 4 hdc, 2 hdc in next hdc) 10 times—60 hdc.

Rnd 8: (Hdc in each of 5 hdc, 2 hdc in next hdc) 10 times—70 hdc.

Rnd 9: (Hdc in each of 6 hdc, 2 hdc in next hdc) 10 times—80 hdc.

Rnd 10: * With G, hdc in 10 sts; cut G; with O, working over G and O ends, hdc in 10 sts; cut O; with B, working over O and B ends, hdc in 10 sts; cut B; with H, working over B and H ends, hdc in 10 sts; cut H. Repeat from * once; sl st in first hdc of rnd. End off.

Rnd 11: Sk first 4 sts of last rnd. Join G in next st, ch 2 for first hdc, hdc in next 9 sts; cutting and working over ends as before, work

10 O hdc, 10 B hdc, 10 H hdc, 10 G hdc, 10 O hdc, 10 B hdc, 10 H hdc. Sl st in first st. End off.

Rnds 12–29: Repeat rnd 11.

Rnd 30: Join G in first st, ch 4, sk 1 st, dc in next st, * ch 2, sk 2 sts, dc in next st, repeat from * around, end ch 2, sl st in 2nd ch of ch 4. End off.

Drawstrings (make 2): With all 4 colors tog, ch 70. End off. Pull drawstring through rnd 30, sew ends of drawstring tog securely. Beg and ending at opposite side of bag, repeat with 2nd drawstring.

Aztec Tote

SIZE: 13″ × 18″.

MATERIALS: Rug yarn, 3 60-yd. skeins each of peacock and gold, 1 skein each of brick, orange, and pink. Crochet hook, size J (6 mm). Large yarn needle.

GAUGE: 3 sc = 1″; 3 rows = 1″

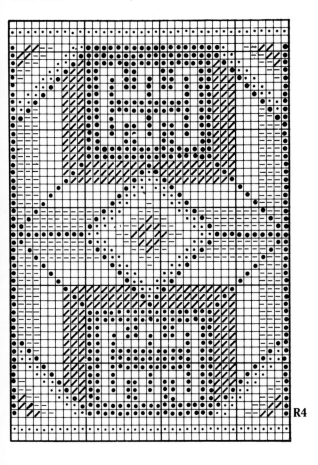

R4

Aztec Tote

TOTE: With gold, ch 38.

Row 1: Sc in 2nd ch from hook and in each ch across—37 sc. Cut yarn. Turn.

Row 2: With pink, make lp on hook, sc in each sc across. Cut yarn. Turn.

Row 3: With gold, repeat row 2.

Row 4 (wrong side): Following chart, with peacock, sc in first sc, drop yarn toward you; with gold, sc in next sc; working over gold strand, with brick, sc in 2 sc, drop yarn toward you; with orange, sc in 2 sc, drop yarn toward you; with gold (carried along from 2nd st), sc in 2 sc, drop yarn toward you; with pink, sc in 2 sc, drop yarn toward you; with peacock, sc in 17 sc, drop yarn toward you; with pink, sc in 2 sc, drop yarn toward you; with gold, sc in 2 sc, working over gold strand, with orange, sc in 2 sc, drop yarn toward you; with brick, sc in 2 sc, drop yarn toward you; with gold (carried along from last gold st), sc in next sc, cut gold; with peacock, sc in last sc. Ch 1, turn.

Continue to work from chart, cutting and joining colors as necessary. Work over yarn ends to hide them. When 2 sections of the same color are close tog, carry color along by working over it from one section to another. Use separate balls of yarn for sections that are more than a few sts apart. Always drop colors that will be used in the next row to the wrong side of work. End off when top of chart is reached.

Make another piece the same. Sew pieces tog along sides and bottom with colors to match edges.

Shell Edging: With brick, make lp on hook; sc in seam at top of bag, * sk 2 sc, 4 dc in next sc, sk 2 sc, sc in next sc, repeat from * around, join in first sc. End off.

Drawstring: With pink, make a chain 45″ long. Beg and ending at center top of bag, run chain through last pink rnd.

☐	Gold
⊡	Pink
▨	Brick
⊟	Orange
▣	Peacock

Shoulder Strap: Using all 5 colors tog, ch 75. Sew ends of chain to side seams of bag.

Shopping Bag Tote

SIZE: 14″ long, 11½″ wide.

MATERIALS: Rug yarn, 4 60-yd. skeins gold (A), 1 skein brick (B), 1 skein peacock (C). Crochet hook size J (6 mm). Large yarn needle.

GAUGE: 3 sts = 1″, 7 rows = 2″.

TOTE

Plain Motif (make 10): With A, ch 11.

Row 1: Sc in 2nd ch from hook and in each ch across—10 sc. Ch 1, turn.

Row 2 (Knit St): Work loosely. Insert hook between 2 vertical bars of sc (not under the 2 horizontal bars in the usual way), pull up a lp, yo and through 2 lps on hook, * work sc in same way between 2 vertical bars of next sc, repeat from * across. Ch 1, turn.

Rows 3–15: Repeat row 2. Do not turn at end of row 15. Ch 1, sl st in each row on side, ch 1, sl st in each ch across bottom edge, ch 1, sl st in each row to top, ch 1, sl st in each st across top. Join; end off.

Striped Motif (make 8): With A, ch 11.

Row 1: Sc in 2nd ch from hook and in each ch across, finish last 2 lps of last sc with C. Cut A. With C, ch 1, turn.

Row 2: Work in knit st as for plain motif, change to B. Cut C. With B, ch 1, turn.

Rows 3–15: Repeat row 2, alternating 1 row B, 1 row A, 1 row C. With A, work sl st around motif.

With A, sew 5 plain and 4 striped motifs tog in checkerboard fashion for front of bag, sewing through back lps of sl sts. Repeat for back of bag. Sew front and back tog on sides and bottom.

HANDLE (make 2): With A, ch 41.

Row 1: Sc in 2nd ch from hook and in each ch across—40 sc. Ch 1, turn.

Rows 2 and 3: Work in knit st. Work sl st in each st around handle. Sew handles in place.

Mother Goose Dolls

These seven individual characters or groups of figures from the pages of Mother Goose come alive with tiny props to illustrate their rhymes. All are made in single and double crochet.

Little Miss Muffett

Three Men in a Tub

Jack Be Nimble

Mary Quite Contrary

Jack and Jill

Little Jack Horner

Little Boy Blue

SIZE: 7″ high.

MATERIALS: Knitting worsted weight yarn, 1 oz. main color for boy figures, 1½ ozs. for girl figures; small amounts of other colors. Crochet hooks, sizes F and H. Tapestry needle. Polyester stuffing.

GAUGE: 4 sc = 1″; 4 rows = 1″ (size F hook)

Note: Use size F hook unless otherwise indicated.

Basic Patterns

BOY

BOY'S HEAD: With pink ch 2.

Rnd 1: 6 sc in 2nd ch from hook. Do not join rnds; mark end of rnds.

Rnd 2: 2 sc in each sc around—12 sc.

Rnd 3: (Sc in next sc, 2 sc in next sc) 6 times—18 sc.

Rnds 4–8: Work even in sc.

Rnd 9: (Sk next sc, sc in next sc) 6 times. Stuff head loosely. Continue to dec 1 sc 4 more times—8 sc. End off.

BOY'S BODY: Beg at bottom, with main color, work as for head through rnd 3.

Rnd 4: (Sc in each of 2 sc, 2 sc in next sc) 6 times—24 sc.

Rnds 5–8: Work even in sc. At end of rnd 8, ch 1, turn.

Bib: Sc in each of 6 sc. Ch 1, turn. Work 3 more rows of 6 sc. End off.

Rnd 9: Beg in next st at end of rnd 8, with shirt color, sc in 18 sc, sc in back lp of next 6 sc (behind bib).

Rnds 10–13: Work even on 24 sc.

Rnd 14: (Sk 1 sc, sc in next 2 sc) 8 times.

Rnd 15: (Sk 1 sc, sc in next sc) 8 times. Stuff loosely.

Rnd 16: (Sc in 2 sc, sk 1 sc) twice, sc in 2 sc—6 sc. End off.

LEG (make 2): Beg at top of leg with main color, ch 9. Join in first ch to form ring.

Rnd 1: Sc in each ch around—9 sc.

Rnds 2–8: Work even in sc.

Rnd 9: With black, sc in back lp of each sc around.

Rnd 10: Sk 1 sc, sc in each sc around—8 sc.

Rnd 11: Sc in each sc around. Ch 1, turn. Sc in each of 3 sc. Ch 1, turn. Work 6 more rows of 3 sc. End off. Fold flap to back of leg forming foot, sew in place, sew sides. Stuff leg loosely.

ARM (make 2): Beg at top of arm with shirt color, ch 7. Join in first ch to form ring.

Rnds 1–7: Work even on 7 sc.

Rnds 8 and 9: With pink, work even.

Rnd 10: Ch 3 (thumb), work even in sc.

Rnds 11 and 12: Work even in sc. End off. Stuff arm loosely; be sure to hold thumb to outside of work.

STRAP (make 2): With main color, ch 12. Sew a ch to each corner of bib, cross straps in back, sew to top of pants.

FINISHING: Sew arms and legs in place, using positions shown in photograph. Thread 20″ of yarn for hair in needle; double yarn. Working from top of head, embroider hair in satin st, making short sts for front, longer sts for back of head. With red, make french knot for mouth. With blue or brown, make french knots for eyes (see *Embroidery Stitches* section at back of book.) Sew cap in place. Sew head in place.

GIRL'S HEAD: Same as for boy.

GIRL'S BODY: With white, work as for boy through rnd 8. Join main color; work sc in each sc around—24 sc.

Beg with rnd 10, work as for boy.

ARM (make 2): Beg at top of arm, with main color, ch 6. Join in first ch to form ring.

Rnds 1–5: Work even in sc.

Rnd 6: Join white; (ch 4, sc in front lp of next 2 sc) 3 times. End off.

Rnd 7: Join pink, sc in back lp of each sc of rnd 5.

Rnds 8 and 9: Work even in sc.

Rnd 10: Ch 4 (thumb), sc in each sc around.

Rnd 11: Work even in sc.

Rnd 12: Sc in next sc, sk 1 sc, sc in next sc. End off. Stuff loosely.

LEG (make 2): With white, ch 8. Join in first ch to form ring.

Rnd 1: Sc in each ch around.

Rnds 2–5: Work even on 8 sc.

Rnd 6: (Ch 4, sc in front lp of next 2 sc) 4 times.

Rnd 7: With black, sc in back lp of each sc of rnd 5.

Rnds 8–10: Work even in sc. At end of rnd 10, ch 1, turn; sc in each of 3 sc. Work even on 3 sc for 5 rows. End off. Fold flap to back of leg, forming foot; sew in place; sew sides. Stuff loosely.

SKIRT: With main color and H hook, ch 20. Join in first ch to form ring.

Rnd 1: Sc in first ch, hdc in next ch, 2 dc in next ch, (dc in each of next 2 ch, 2 dc in next ch) 6 times—26 sts.

Rnd 2: (Dc in each of next 2 sts, 2 dc in next dc) 8 times, dc in each of last 2 dc—34 dc.

Rnd 3: Work even in dc.

Rnd 4: (Dc in each of next 3 sts, 2 dc in next dc) 8 times, dc in each of last 2 dc—42 dc.

Rnds 5–7: Work even in dc. At end of rnd 7, hdc in next st, sc in next st.

Rnd 8: With white, * sc in next st, (sc, ch 4, sc) in next st, repeat from * around. End off.

COLLAR: With white, ch 8. Sc in 2nd ch from hook, * ch 4, sc in same ch, sc in next ch, repeat from * to end. End off.

SASH: Leaving 6″ end, ch 18. End off, leaving 6″ end. Tie around waist with bow in back.

FINISHING: Sew skirt to body. Finish same as for boy.

Little Miss Muffet

Using bright pink for main color, make one girl figure.

BONNET: With main color, ch 2.

Rnd 1: 6 sc in 2nd ch from hook.

Rnd 2: 2 sc in each sc—12 sc.

Rnd 3: (Sc in next sc, 2 sc in next sc) 6 times—18 sc.

Rnd 4: Sc in back lp of next 14 sc. Ch 1, turn.

Rows 5–7: Sc in 14 sc. Ch 1, turn each row.

Row 8: 2 sc in each sc. Ch 1, turn.

Row 9: Sc in each sc. Turn.

Row 10: Join white. Work sc in 2 sc, * ch 4, sc in same sc as last sc, sc in each of next 2 sc, repeat from * across. End off.

TUFFET: With white, ch 12. Work even on 11 sc for 20 rows. End off. Fold in half.

With main color, beg at fold, work side edges tog, working through both thicknesses: * sc in each of 2 sts, ch 4, sc in same st, repeat from * along 2 sides. Stuff loosely. Repeat between *'s on last open side, then work edging across fold. End off. Make french knot at center.

SPIDER: With brown or black yarn (mohair or angora is best), make basic boy's head. Make french knots for eyes and mouth. (See *Embroidery Stitches* Section at back of book.)

LEGS (make 8): Ch 12 very tightly. End off. Tie a knot in end of ch for foot. Sew 4 legs to each side of body.

BOWL: Work as for bonnet through rnd 2. Work 3 rnds in sc. End off.

Jack Be Nimble

Using dark blue for main color and red for shirt, make basic boy figure.

CAP: With main color, ch 2.

Rnd 1: 6 sc in 2nd ch from hook.

Rnd 2: (2 sc in next sc, sc in next sc) 3 times—9 sc.

Rnd 3: (2 sc in next sc, sc in next sc) 5 times.

Rnds 4–7: Work even on 14 sc.

Rnd 8: 2 sc in back lp of each sc around—28 sc.

Rnds 9 and 10: Work even. End off. Cut 3 pieces of yarn 2″ long. Knot ends tog. Separate strands to form a fluffy feather. Trim. Sew to side of cap.

CANDLESTICK HOLDER: With gray, ch 2.

Rnd 1: 6 sc in 2nd ch from hook.

Rnds 2 and 3: 2 sc in each sc—24 sc.

Rnd 4: Sc in back lp of each sc.

Rnd 5: Work even in sc. Ch 1, turn.

HANDLE: Sc in 2 sc. Ch 1, turn. Work 12 rows on 2 sc. End off. Sew handle in place.

CANDLE: With red, ch 5. Join to form ring. Work even on 5 sc for 1½″. Join yellow; sk 1 sc, work 2 rnds on 4 sc. End off. Sew candle to holder.

Jack And Jill

JACK: Make one basic boy figure with brown for main color, yellow for shirt.

CAP: Work as for Jack Be Nimble's cap through rnd 6.

Rnds 7–9: Work as for rnds 8–10.

JILL: Make one basic girl figure with yellow for main color.

SKIRT: Work basic skirt through rnd 4.

Rnd 5: (Dc in each of 3 sts, 2 dc in next dc) 10 times, hdc in next st, sc in next st. Work rnd 8 of basic skirt.

BONNET: With white, ch 2.

Rnd 1: 6 sc in 2nd ch from hook.

Rnd 2: 2 sc in each sc—12 sc.

Rnd 3: 2 dc in each sc—24 dc.

Rnd 4: Work even in dc.

Rnd 5: (Sk 1 dc, sc in each of next 2 dc) 8 times.

Rnd 6: * Ch 4, sc in same st, sc in each of next 2 sc, repeat from * around. End off.

PAIL: With gray, ch 2.

Rnd 1: 6 sc in 2nd ch from hook.

Rnd 2: 2 sc in each sc around—12 sc.

Rnd 3: Sc in back lp of each sc around.

Rnd 4: (Sc in 3 sc, 2 sc in next sc) 3 times.

Rnds 5 and 6: Work even on 15 sc.

Rnd 7: (Sc in 4 sc, 2 sc in next sc) 3 times.

Rnd 8: Work even on 18 sc.

Rnd 9: (Sc in 5 sc, 2 sc in next sc) 3 times.

Rnd 10: Work even on 21 sc. Sl st in next st. Ch 15. Sew in place for handle.

Little Boy Blue

Using blue for main color, white for shirt, follow basic pattern for boy's head and body.

LEG: Follow basic pattern through rnd 8.

Rnd 9: With pink, sc in back lp of each sc around.

Rnd 10: Sk 1 sc, sc in each sc around.

Rnd 11: Sc in 8 sc. Ch 1, turn.

Row 12: Sc in 3 sc. Ch 1, turn.

Row 13: Sc in 3 sc. Ch 5 (toe), turn.

Row 14: Sc in 3 sc. Ch 1, turn.

Row 15: Sc in 2 sc, sc in back lp of next sc (behind toe), ch 1, turn. Work 3 more rows of 3 sc. End off. Fold foot to back of leg so that toe is out. Sew in place. Stuff.
   Work left leg the same through rnd 11.

Row 12: Sc in 3 sc. Ch 4 (toe), turn.

Row 13: Sc in 3 sc. Ch 1, turn.

Row 14: Sc in 2 sc, sc in back lp of next sc. Ch 1, turn. Finish as for right foot.

ARM: Work as for basic pattern through rnd 7. End off. With pink, ch 6. Join to form ring.

Rnd 1: Sc in each ch around.

Rnds 2–4: Work even in sc.

Rnd 5: Ch 4 (thumb), sc in each sc.

Rnds 6 and 7: Work even in sc. End off. Sew arms to sleeves at right angles.

CAP: Beg at top, with main color, ch 2.

Rnd 1: 6 sc in 2nd ch from hook.

Rnds 2 and 3: 2 sc in each sc around—24 sc.

Rnds 4–6: Work even.

Rnd 7: Sc in front lp of each sc.

Rnd 8: (Sc in 2 sc, 2 sc in next sc) 8 times.

Rnds 9–11: Work even on 32 sc. End off.

HORN: Ch 8. Sc in 2nd ch from hook and in each of next 5 ch, 10 dc in last ch. End off. Sew side seam. Ch 8; sew on for handle.

HAYSTACK: Beg at bottom, with yellow and H hook, ch 4. Join to form ring.

Rnd 1: 6 sc in ring.

Rnd 2: 2 dc in each sc around.

Rnd 3: 2 dc in each dc around—24 dc.

Rnd 4: (Dc in 2 dc, 2 dc in next dc) 8 times.

Rnd 5: (Dc in 2 dc, 2 dc in next dc) 10 times, dc in 2 dc—42 dc.

Rnd 6: Working in back lps, (dc in 4 dc, sk 1 dc) 8 times, dc in 2 dc.

Rnd 7: Cut a strip of cardboard 2″ wide. * Holding strip in front of work, wrap yarn around cardboard once, dc in next dc, repeat from * around.

Rnd 8: (Dc in 4 dc, sk next dc) 6 times, dc in 4 dc.

Rnd 9: Repeat rnd 7.

Rnd 10: Work in dc, sk every 5th st.

Rnds 11–16: Repeat rnds 7 and 10 alternately. Stuff loosely.

Rnd 17: Repeat rnd 7.

Rnd 18: (Dc in 2 dc, sk 1 dc) 4 times.

Rnd 19: Repeat rnd 7. End off. Sew up top.

Three Men In A Tub

Make 3 basic boy figures using different colors for each.

BUTCHER'S CAP: Beg at center top, ch 2.

Rnd 1: 6 sc in 2nd ch from hook.

Rnd 2: 2 sc in each sc around—12 sc.

Rnd 3: (Sc in next sc, 2 sc in next sc) 6 times—18 sc.

Rnd 4: Sc in back lp of each sc.

Rnds 5–7: Work even. At end of rnd 7, ch 1, turn.

Rows 8 and 9: Sc in 6 sc. Ch 1, turn.

Row 10: Sk 1 sc, sc in 4 sc, sl st in next sc. End off.

BAKER'S CAP: Beg at center top, ch 2.

Rnd 1: 6 sc in 2nd ch from hook.

Rnd 2: 2 sc in each sc around—12 sc.

Rnds 3–5: (Sc in next sc, 2 sc in next sc) around—40 sc.

Rnd 6: (2 sc in next sc, sc in next 2 sc) 13 times, 2 sc in next sc—54 sc.

Rnd 7: Dc in each sc around—54 dc.

Rnd 8: (Sk next dc, sc in next dc) 27 times—27 sc.

Rnd 9: (Sk next sc, sc in next 2 sc) 9 times.

Rnd 10: Sc in front lp of each sc around.

Rnds 11 and 12: Work even on 18 sc. End off.

CANDLESTICK MAKER'S CAP: Beg at center top, ch 2.

Rnd 1: 6 sc in 2nd ch from hook.

Rnds 2–5: (Sc in next sc, 2 sc in next sc) around—27 sc.

Rnd 6: Work even in sc.

Rnd 7: Sc in front lp of each sc.

Rnd 8: Work even in sc. End off.

TUB: Beg at center, ch 2.

Rnd 1: 6 sc in 2nd ch from hook.

Rnds 2–4: 2 dc in each st around—48 dc.

Rnd 5: (Dc in next 2 dc, 2 dc in next dc) 16 times—64 dc.

Rnd 6: (Dc in next 4 dc, 2 dc in next dc) 12 times—76 dc.

Rnd 7: Dc in back lp of each dc around.

Rnds 8 and 9: Work even in dc.

Rnd 10: (Dc in 10 dc, sk 1 dc) 6 times, dc in 10 dc. End off.

HANDLE (make 2): Ch 12. Sc in 2nd ch from hook and in each remaining ch. End off. Sew in place.

Mary, Mary Quite Contrary

Make basic girl figure.

BONNET: Work same as body through rnd 5—24 sc.

Rnd 6: (Sk 1 sc, sc in 5 sc) 4 times—20 sc. Ch 1, turn.

Row 7: Sk first sc, 2 sc in each of next 15 sc—30 sc. Ch 1, turn.

Row 8: Sk first sc, sc in 29 sc. Ch 1, turn.

Row 9: Sk first sc, sc in 28 sc. Cut main color. Turn.

Row 10: Join white, sc in 2nd sc, sc in next sc, * ch 4, sc in same sc, sc in each of next 2 sc, repeat from * across. End off.

WATERING CAN: Ch 2; 8 sc in 2nd ch from hook. Sc in front lp of each sc around. Ch 4, work 6 sc in 2nd ch from hook, sc in each of next 2 ch (spout). Work 4 more rnds of sc on can, holding spout to outside of work. End off. Sew side seam of spout.
Ch 10 for handle. Sew in place.

FLOWERS (make 3)

Pot: Work as for head through rnd 2. Sc in back lp of each sc around. Work even for 2 rnds. End off.

Stem: With green, ch 8. Sc in 2nd ch from hook, sc in each of next 2 ch. Ch 4 for leaf, sc in same sc, sc in each of last 4 ch. End off. Sew side seam of stem.

Flower: With bright color, ch 2. Work 6 sc in 2nd ch from hook. (Ch 4, sc in next sc) 5 times. End off. Sew flower to stem, sew stem to bottom of pot.

Little Jack Horner

Make a basic boy figure.

CAP: Ch 2.

Rnd 1: 6 sc in 2nd ch from hook.

Rnds 2 and 3: (2 sc in next sc, sc in next sc) 8 times.

Rnds 4–7: Work even on 14 sc.

Rnd 8: 2 sc in back lp of each sc around—28 sc.

Rnds 9 and 10: Work even. End off. For hatband, ch 18; sew in place.

PIE PAN: With gray, ch 2.

Rnd 1: 6 sc in 2nd ch from hook.

Rnd 2: 2 sc in each sc—12 sc.

Rnds 3–5: (Sc in 2 sc, 2 sc in next sc) around—28 sc.

Rnd 6: Sc in back lp of each sc.

Rnd 7: Sc in each sc. End off.

PIE CRUST: With tan, ch 2.

Rnd 1: 6 sc in 2nd ch from hook.

Rnds 2 and 3: 2 sc in each sc—24 sc.

Rnd 4: (Sc in next sc, 2 sc in next sc) 12 times—36 sc.

Rnd 5: Work even in sc.

Rnd 6: (Sc in 2 sc, ch 4, sc in same sc) around. End off. Sew crust to pie pan, stuffing before closing opening.

PLUM (make 2): With dark red, ch 2; 4 sc in 2nd ch from hook, sc in each sc around. End off. Sew one plum to thumb, one to top of pie.

GENERAL DIRECTIONS

How to Knit

Knitting is based on two stitches, the knit stitch and the purl stitch. Many knitted sweaters and accessories can be made with these two stitches alone. Before starting any knitted piece, it is necessary to cast on a certain number of stitches; that is, to place a series of loops on one needle so that you can work your first row of knitting. After you have finished a piece of knitting, it is necessary to bind off the stitches so that they will not unravel.

CASTING ON: There are many ways of casting on stitches. The method shown here is only one of them. It gives you a strong and elastic edge.

Step 1: Allow enough yarn for the number of stitches to be cast on (about ½" per stitch for lighter weight yarns such as baby yarns, 1" per stitch for heavier yarns such as knitting worsted, more for bulky yarns on large needles). Make a slip loop on needle, as shown above, and tighten knot gently.

Step 2: Hold needle in right hand with short end of yarn over left thumb. Weave strand that comes from ball through right hand, over index finger, under second, over third and under fourth finger.

Step 3: Bring needle forward to make a loop over left thumb. Insert needle from left to right in loop; bring yarn in right hand under, then over point of needle and draw yarn through loop with tip of needle.

Step 4: Keeping right hand in same position, tighten stitch on needle gently with left hand. You now have 2 stitches on needle. Repeat Steps 3 and 4 for required number of stitches.

KNIT STITCH

Step 1: Hold needle with cast on stitches in left hand and yarn in same position as for casting on in right hand. Insert point of needle from left to right in first stitch.

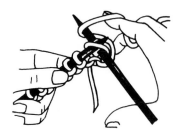

Step 2: Bring yarn under and over point of right needle.

Step 3: Draw yarn through stitch with point of needle.

Step 4: Allow loop on left needle to slip off needle. Loop on right needle is your first knit stitch. Repeat from Figure 5 in each loop across row. When you have finished knitting one row, place needle with stitches in left hand ready to start next row.

GARTER STITCH: Knit every row to make the garter stitch.

PURL STITCH

To purl, insert needle from right to left in stitch on left needle. Bring yarn over and under point of right needle. Draw yarn back through stitch and allow loop on left needle to slip off needle.

STOCKINETTE STITCH: Alternate knit and purl rows to work the stockinette stitch.

Purl Side

Knit Side

BINDING OFF: Knit the first two stitches. Insert left needle from left to right through front of first stitch. Lift first stitch over second stitch and over tip of right needle. One stitch has been bound off, and one stitch remains on right needle. Knit another stitch. Again lift first stitch on right needle over second stitch and off right needle. Continue across until all stitches have been bound off. One loop remains on right needle. Cut yarn, pull end through loop and tighten knot.

INCREASING ONE STITCH

Method 1

Method 1: Knit 1 stitch in the usual way but do not slip it off left needle. Bring right needle behind left needle, insert it from right to left in same stitch (called "the back of the stitch") and make another knit stitch. Slip stitch off left needle.

To increase 1 stitch on the purl stitch, purl 1 stitch but do not slip it off left needle. Bring yarn between needles to back, knit 1 stitch in back of same stitch.

Method 2: Pick up horizontal strand between stitch just knitted and next stitch, place it on left needle. Knit 1 stitch in back of this strand, thus twisting it.

Method 3: Place right needle behind left needle. Insert right needle in stitch below next stitch, knit this stitch, then knit stitch above it in the usual way.

DECREASING ONE STITCH

On the right side of work, knit 2 stitches together as in illustration, through the front of the stitches (the decrease slants to the right), or through the back of the stitches (the decrease slants to the left). On the purl side, purl 2 stitches together. Another decrease stitch is called "psso" (pass slip stitch over). When directions say "sl 1, k 1, psso", slip first stitch (take it from left to right needle without knitting it), knit next stitch, then bring slip stitch over knit as in binding off.

CASTING ON AT BEGINNING OF ROW

Step 1: Draw a loop of yarn through first stitch as if to knit.

Step 2: Pull loop onto right needle.

Step 3: Turn loop and place it on left needle as shown. One stitch has been cast on. Without removing right needle, repeat from Figure 1 for required number of cast-on stitches.

CHECKING YOUR GAUGE: Before starting any knitted or crocheted garment, be sure you can work to the exact gauge specified in the directions. To test your knit gauge, cast on 20 to 30 stitches, using needles suggested. Work 3″ in pattern stitch. Smooth out swatch, pin down. Measure across 2″ counting number of stitches; measure 2″ down counting number of rows. If you have more stitches and rows to the inch than directions specify, you are working too tightly. Use larger needles. If you have fewer stitches and rows to the inch, you are working too loosely. Use smaller needles. Knit new swatches until gauge is correct. Test crochet in same way.

BLOCKING: Smooth pieces out, wrong side up, on a padded surface. Using rustproof pins, place pins at top and bottom of each piece, measuring to insure correct length. Pin sides of pieces to correct width. Place pins all around outer edges, keeping patterns straight. Do not pin ribbings.

Flat pressing technique (for stockinette stitch, flat rows of crochet, and other smooth surfaces): Cover with damp cloth. Lower iron gently, allowing steam to penetrate knitted or crocheted fabric. Do not press down hard or hold iron in one place long enough to dry out pressing cloth. Do not slide iron over surface.

Steaming technique (for mohair and other fluffy yarns and raised pattern stitches): Support weight of iron in your hand; hold as close as possible to piece without touching it and move slowly over entire piece, making sure steam penetrates completely. If yarn is extra heavy, use a spray iron or wet pressing cloth to provide extra steam. When blocked pieces are dry, remove pins and sew garment together. Steam-press seams from wrong side, using a steam iron or damp cloth and dry iron and same blocking method.

KNITTING ABBREVIATIONS

k–knit	psso–pass slip stitch over
p–purl	inc–increase
st–stitch	dec–decrease
sts–stitches	beg–beginning
yo–yarn over	pat–pattern
sl–slip	lp–loop
sk–skip	MC–main color
tog–together	CC–contrasting color
rnd–round	dp–double-pointed

How to Crochet

All crochet work begins with a chain, a series of loops made by pulling yarn through a loop on your crochet hook to make a new loop.

Many beautiful and intricate patterns can be made in crochet, most of them a variation of a few basic stitches that are illustrated here—chain stitch, single crochet, double crochet, and slip stitch.

CHAIN STITCH: To make first loop on hook, grasp yarn about 2″ from end between left thumb and index finger. With right hand, lap long strand over short end, forming a loop.

Hold loop in place with left thumb and index finger. Grasp hook in right hand, insert hook through loop, catch strand with hook and draw it through loop. Pull end and long strand in opposite directions to close loop around hook.

Step 1: To make your first chain stitch, pass hook under yarn on index finger and catch strand with hook.

Draw yarn through loop on hook. This makes one chain stitch. Repeat last step until you have as many chains as you need. One loop always remains on hook. Practice making all chains uniform.

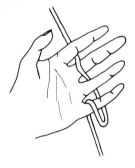

Step 2: Weave yarn through left hand.

SINGLE CROCHET

Step 1: Insert hook in second chain from hook. Yarn over hook.

Step 2: Draw yarn through chain. Two loops on hook.

Step 3: Yarn over hook. Draw yarn through 2 loops on hook. One single crochet has been made.

Step 4: Work a single crochet in each chain stitch. At end of row, chain 1 and turn work around.

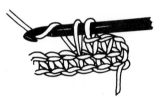

Step 5: Insert hook under both top loops of first stitch, yarn over hook and draw through stitch. Yarn over and through 2 loops on hook. Work a single crochet in same way in each stitch across row.

INCREASING 1 SINGLE CROCHET: To increase 1 single crochet, work 2 stitches in 1 stitch.

DECREASING 1 SINGLE CROCHET: To decrease 1 single crochet, pull up a loop in 1 stitch, pull up a loop in next stitch (3 loops on hook), yarn over hook, draw through all 3 loops at once.

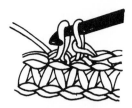

SLIP STITCH: Insert hook in work. Yarn over hook and draw through both the stitch and the loop on hook. The slip stitch makes a firm finishing edge. A single slip stitch is used for joining a chain to form a ring.

HALF DOUBLE CROCHET

Step 1: Yarn over hook. Insert hook in 3rd chain from hook.

Step 2: Yarn over hook, draw through chain. Yarn over hook again.

Step 3: Draw through all 3 loops on hook. One half double crochet has been made.

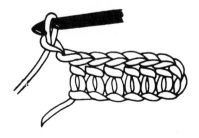

Step 4: Work a half double crochet in each chain across. At end of row, ch 2 and turn work.

DOUBLE CROCHET

Step 1: Yarn over hook. Insert hook in 4th chain from hook.

Step 2: Yarn over hook. Draw through chain. There are 3 loops on hook.

Step 3: Yarn over hook. Draw through 2 loops on hook. There are 2 loops on hook. Yarn over hook.

Step 4: Draw yarn through remaining 2 loops on hook. One double crochet has been made. When you have worked a double crochet in each chain across, chain 3 and turn work. In most directions, the turning chain 3 counts as first double crochet of next row. In working the 2nd row, skip the first stitch and work a double crochet in the 2 top loops of each double crochet across. The last double crochet of each row is worked in the top chain of the chain 3 turning chain.

TREBLE OR TRIPLE CROCHET: With 1 loop on hook put yarn over hook twice, insert in 5th chain from hook, pull loop through. Yarn over and draw through 2 loops at a time 3 times. At end of a row, chain 4 and turn. Chain 4 counts as first treble of next row.

TURNING CROCHET WORK: In crochet a certain number of ch sts are needed at the end of each row to bring work into position for the next row. Then work is turned so reverse side is facing the crocheter. Follow the stitch table below for the number of ch sts to make a turn.

Single crochet (sc)	Ch 1 to turn
Half double crochet (half dc or hdc)	Ch 2 to turn
Double crochet (dc)	Ch 3 to turn
Treble crochet (tr)	Ch 4 to turn
Double treble crochet (dtr)	Ch 5 to turn
Treble treble crochet (tr tr)	Ch 6 to turn

ENDING OFF: When last loop of finished piece is reached, cut yarn end leaving several inches. Pull the end through the loop and thread it through a tapestry needle. Weave the yarn back into the work below the top row of stitches for an inch or two and cut off the excess.

FOLLOWING DIRECTIONS: An asterisk (*) is often used in crochet directions to indicate repetition. For example, when directions read "* 2 dc in next st, 1 dc in next st, repeat from * 4 times" this means to work directions after first * until second * is reached, then go back to first * 4 times more. Work 5 times in all.

When parentheses () are used to show repetition, work directions within parentheses as many times as specified. For example, "(dc, ch 1) 3 times" means to do what is within () 3 times altogether.

"Work even" in directions means to work in same stitch without increasing or decreasing.

CHECKING YOUR GAUGE: See *How to Knit* section.

BLOCKING: See *How to Knit* section.

CROCHET ABBREVIATIONS

ch–chain stitch	sc–single crochet
st–stitch	sl st–slip stitch
sts–stitches	dc–double crochet
lp–loop	hdc–half double crochet
inc–increase	tr–treble or triple crochet
dec–decrease	dtr–double treble crochet
rnd–round	tr tr–treble treble crochet
beg–beginning	bl–block
sk–skip	sp–space
p–picot	pat–pattern
tog–together	yo–yarn over hook

Yarn Source Guide

Manos de Uruguay   MANOS YARNS
35 West 36th Street
New York, NY 10018

Merino Wool   MERINO WOOL CO., INC.
230 Fifth Avenue
New York, NY 10001

Embroidery Stitches

Satin Stitch

Straight Stitch

French Knot

Lazy Daisy Stitch

Cross-Stitch